long

as you

write

About Dear Damsels

Dear Damsels is a platform and community publishing empowering collections of fiction, non-fiction and poetry, and supporting women writers through free and inclusive submission opportunities.

WWW.DEARDAMSELS.COM

About Kerry Ryan

Kerry Ryan writes plays, poetry and prose. She has won the Spilling Ink Short Story Prize and has been published in *The Manchester Review*, *The Kenyon Review*, *3am Magazine* among others. She is the founder of Write like a Grrrl, which is now taught across the globe, and Collectivity – a collective for experienced and emerging writers. She has facilitated creative workshops for the STUC, Sothebys, Spotlight, New Queers and many others.

She has an MLitt and a PhD in Literary Studies & Creative Writing.

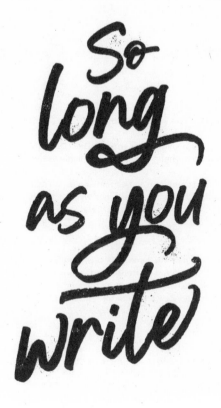

Women on writing

Edited by Kerry Ryan

First published in Great Britain in 2022 by Dear Damsels

Compilation copyright © Dear Damsels
Individual copyright retained by the respective contributors

The right of the contributors to be identified as the Authors of the Work
has been asserted by them in accordance with the Copyright, Designs and
Patents Act 1988.

1

Apart from any use permitted under UK copyright law, this publication may
only be reproduced, stored, or transmitted, in any form, or by any means,
with prior permission in writing of the publishers or, in the case of reprographic
production, in accordance with the terms of licences issued by the Copyright
Licensing Agency.

ISBN 978-1-8381-6612-0

Printed and bound in Great Britain by Clays Ltd, Elcograf S.p.A.

Dear Damsels
www.deardamsels.com

Dear Damsels gratefully acknowledges that our work is supported using
public funding by Arts Council England.

Supported using public funding by
**ARTS COUNCIL
ENGLAND**

'So long as you write what you wish to write, that is all that matters; and whether it matters for ages or only for hours, nobody can say.'

Virginia Woolf,
A Room of One's Own

Contents

CHAPTER 1

How to be a Writer

CHAPTER 3

Inner Critic

CHAPTER 4

Writing
Practice

CHAPTER 5

Be
Courageous

A letter from Dear Damsels

We're sure that many of you, at times, have believed you had nothing to say. It's an easy feeling to develop – a thought bubbling away as you sit silent in a classroom, as you are talked down in an argument, or swatted away mid-sentence in a meeting, told to be quiet, wait your turn, let someone else speak first.

Swallowing your words, waiting patiently to blurt out a 'sorry, but—' or deciding it's not worth the hassle: these are the kinds of all-too-common experiences that make us feel like we cannot speak up; that our stories aren't worth anything.

In 2016, we created Dear Damsels out of the belief that women can overcome these feelings and find their voice through the act of writing. While we didn't believe someone's words had to be published in order to matter, we had the feeling that one woman sharing her words might just inspire another to do the same.

This book is an invitation for you to do just that – to be encouraged by the stories, essays and poems that these women writers have shared, and to feel empowered to share your own.

We always set out to create collections that readers will cherish and return to, but this is especially true of *So Long As You Write*. We like to think that this book will find a home on your desk. Perhaps you will tuck it alongside your notebook, there to dip into whenever you're in need of inspiration, support or encouragement.

We hope it will be a reminder that your voice will always matter.

Abby & Bridie
Co-founders of Dear Damsels

A letter from
Kerry Ryan

You now hold a community of women in your hands. This is your community. A place of refuge, a safe space to retreat to when times are tough and the words won't come. When energy is waning and hope dips, open this book and hear these voices sing. This unique anthology of essays, stories and poetry contains songs of protest, resistance and resilience that harmonise into a collective roar: *you can do it*.

So Long as You Write is the kind of collection I longed for when I began writing. Instead, what I had to do was gather together the essays and interviews, the poetry and prose of the feminist authors I loved and save them into one big doc on my MacBook. It was messy and rough, but it was a resource I could turn to in times of need. Those women told me I had a right to write. They told me my voice mattered. They told me that a word after a word was power. They told me that all I had to do was keep writing, keep reading, and one day it would get easier. They told me there would be joy. And they were right.

I raised a community on the foundation of those women's words. I took everything I learned and passed it on to my students, and as those students developed in their own practice, their words, their grace and determination encouraged and inspired me. Women supporting women supporting women. Which is exactly what you'll find in this collective of voices you now hold.

At the heart of everything that Write like a Grrrl – the collective of writers I founded – and Dear Damsels do, is community. This collaboration stands testament to that passion and commitment. Yes, writing is a solitary act. Yes, it can be difficult and frustrating. But community can offer the spiritual support we need. If writing is an act of faith, others help us believe. Others help us take the leap. When we are alone, we can get lost, carried away with our own thoughts and fears. In community, we see aspects of our own lives reflected back to us and it gives us strength. It gives us hope. We are emboldened.

In this collection, you'll find four sections: How to be a Writer; Finding your Voice; The Inner Critic; and Being Courageous. You'll discover writing that is imaginative, moving and often funny as hell. These stories, poems and essays track the whole spectrum of the writing life from the highs to the lows, from page to the stage and to the shelves of Waterstones. They demonstrate how courage is not the absence of fear but the capacity to move ahead in spite of fear.

Throughout the anthology, you'll also find my writing tips. Perhaps the most important is: *Be an authority.* In my experience, this is what we struggle with the most. And is it any wonder? Globally, women are paid less, promoted less, expected to carry the burden of unpaid caregiving, have their reproductive rights controlled, are more likely to experience sexual harassment and domestic violence and to live in poverty with less access to education. And this is before factoring in class, race, ethnicity and disability. There are too many countries where women don't have equal legal standing in a court of law. Being an authority is not the norm.

This is why your words matter. Each story you write, every poem and essay, is a song of protest, no matter which key it's sung in or the form it takes. Writing is rebellion. It's a political act, a refusal to be silenced. So write. Be an authority. Keep this book by your bedside table or your desk to pick up whenever you waver. Come close. Closer. Put your ear to the page and listen. Hear your community sing.

Kerry Ryan,
Editor

CHAPTER 1

How to
be a
Writer

Inspiration and the Process

LUAN GOLDIE

I'm a normal person from a working-class background with a family and job. But in 2019 I also became a published author. My debut *Nightingale Point* was released on the hottest day of the decade and came with a lot of hype. It had media coverage, strong sales and was longlisted for some very nice prizes. People wanted to talk to me about it, about the inspirations behind the characters and the shocking true-life event that inspired the novel itself. People also wanted to ask me about my *writing process*.

I found it so funny, because I wasn't aware that a process was something I was meant to have in order to be a writer. I thought I just needed words. I wasn't quite sure what people meant by 'process' either. Were they expecting me to tell them that I could only write at my walnut desk, with an aged whiskey on one side, scented candle on the other? Why did anyone care about my process anyway?

Having given it some thought, I understand why people are curious about how writers 'do it' – how we sit there alone in silence for hours, days, years, and make stuff up. Sometimes I say: 'It just comes to me.' It doesn't. Writing is bloody hard work. So to you, reader who wants to write, I say the following...

What you need

When I first started writing, I did try to emulate *real writers*, meaning I grabbed a Moleskine notebook and marched myself off to the nearest coffee shop. However, I live in east London and the local Costa is full of people shouting into their phones, eating tuna pasta salads and openly discussing credit card scams. It was all too distracting. Plus, I had to pay £2.10 each time I wanted a cup of tea. So that was out. As were writing retreats (too expensive), the local library (because it was louder than Costa) and my second home (because I don't have one).

So now I am a real writer who writes at home in the living room, at the same table my family eats our meals at. Over time I've got more bougie, adding a desk chair from Argos and a back-saving laptop stand and keyboard. But a special desk? No. An office? Hell, no.

There's no magic. There's no muse. There's just me, often shivering under a blanket wearing fingerless gloves and binge-eating banana chips.

The truth is I don't need much to write – and I believe that if you want to write, you should start by telling yourself that you don't need much either. There are so many barriers to writing

– don't build another by telling yourself you can only do it in a particular coffee shop or with a specific pen. And if anyone tells you that you need a room of your own, a silent log cabin or an intensive writing course costing thousands of pounds, simply ignore them. Sure, those things are helpful – but trust me, you can write without them.

First drafts

So, about that process. Over time, I've realised I do write in a certain way. Personally, I always start with character and dialogue because this is what comes to me first. The characters and their conversations are my inspiration. In my second novel, *Homecoming*, a story that explores family ties and female friendships in the face of loss, one of the main characters is Kiama. When I started thinking about him, he was already fully formed. It was like he already existed – I could see him as a pale, agitated baby, then as an eight-year-old with messy plaits licking melted ice cream off his arm. I saw him as a lost and pampered eighteen-year-old in a Supreme t-shirt, bickering with his dad about gardening. I could see him, smell him, hear him speak, the way he sometimes dragged his words out in a whine and used council estate slang even though he grew up in the suburbs. I felt I knew him inside out, but to find out what happened to him I had to start writing . . . because I was desperate to know that too.

When I start writing, I have very little idea what's going to happen. Yet some writers can't write without first plotting every chapter and smoothing out every plot point. We're all different.

My first draft is around fifty thousand words of dialogue and it's pretty bad – full of misspellings and no punctuation.

Characters have strange names that change throughout and there is zero continuity; it might be snowing one day and there's a picnic the next, and the whole thing is littered with notes in block capitals like IS HITCHAM A REAL PLACE? and IS HE SEXY OR WEIRD? With these drafts nothing really makes sense. But the more I hear the characters talk and see how they interact with each other, the more I understand the story. It's like a gradual unveiling, scene by scene, until the whole picture is revealed.

Writing this way is probably quite inefficient, but it's what works for me. And it doesn't matter how many podcasts I listen to where some bestseller breaks down how they knock out a novel in six weeks, or when a writer I admire explains how to plot using coloured Post-its – whenever I've tried any of those things it simply hasn't worked. The writing is no better and I'm left feeling like I've failed at something others find so easy.

Also, while we're on first drafts, yes, they are meant to be shit.

Nothing is wasted

While novels are my thing, winning the Costa Short Story Award was how I got a publisher's attention (because publishing houses love prizes – you know those little stickers they put on the front of books to help sell them?). I've always wanted to write novels, whereas I write short stories basically to just torture myself. While I find them so very hard to write they are more rewarding for me to read back. I'm happier when I read one of my short stories than one of my novels. I feel they're as tight as I could make them and there's nothing I haven't wedged, squeezed and prised in there. Whereas with my novels, there's always something I feel I haven't included or explained fully enough. This is true to the extent that

I could write my first novel over again – same plot, different characters. Perhaps one day I will, just for myself.

I don't know how much the two kinds of writing – short stories and novels – feed into each other. They are, for me, as different as fiction and non-fiction. Though sometimes, when I've been ploughing through a novel for months, it's delightful to get back into a short story, to not have to drag around characters and all their issues and trauma for years. And even though I am a very slow writer and will dip in and out of short stories over long periods of time (my current record is six years for a story called 'The Orange Pool'), I'm not actively thinking about those characters or their lives unless the page is open in front of me.

One of my most recent writing-related breakdowns came when I realised the novel I had been working on for months was, in fact, not very interesting or believable. For some reason, I thought I was the kind of writer who was good at plotting and would be able to write a thriller. I was wrong and it was dire.

It hurt to let this project go, to close the document knowing I'd spent all that time on something that would probably never see the light of day. I'm not alone in this. We've all been there and it can be really upsetting if you finally start writing that novel you've been dreaming of, to then discover six months down the line that it's not good enough to be a novel at all.

But maybe it was never a novel in the first place. Perhaps it was always meant to be a novella or a short story. When this happens it's important to remember that nothing is wasted in writing. Even if I junk the whole of my fourth novel there will be something in it, some character trait or plot point, that will find its way into another, better piece of writing.

Finding the time

How busy are you? Do you have life admin and a home to clean? Are you a parent? Do you have a job, a career? Are you a carer? Or are you single with a busy social life? Whatever your situation, it can be hard to first find the time and then to justify the time to write. But we must.

Think about your characters and your stories. Allow your mind to wander. Hold it all in your head until you're desperate to write and then, when you have time, let it all flood out. It might be crap. It probably will be crap. But that doesn't matter. You're only telling yourself the story at this time. Keep writing, keep adding, keep editing, keep refining. Just keep going.

Don't, whatever you do, start thinking that you'll only ever write a novel if you spend money on an expensive writing retreat. Or if you could chuck your job in. Or if you religiously knock out two thousand words a day. But if you have time, write. And you *do* have time. Because even when I was working my day job and trying to figure out how to raise a small child, I still found time to watch *The Real Housewives* and still found time to wash the dishes and still definitely found time to browse ASOS. There is always time somewhere. It's not that watching crap TV or browsing ASOS is bad, it's more that if you want to be a writer, well, you've got to write. That's the bottom line. It's amazing where you can snatch small pockets of time in your day. So much of *Nightingale Point* was drafted in the evenings after work, or when my baby took a nap. And even though by the time I wrote *Homecoming* I was part-time at school, I still had to squeeze in writing around teaching and family, and you'd often find me proofreading in a quiet Year 5 classroom at lunchtime or letting my daughter watch three hours of *The Masked Singer* so I could meet a deadline. Find the minutes, use them, and be smug at the end of the month when you see what you've achieved. Every sentence counts.

The internet

Let's be honest, if you've managed to carve out time and you're sitting at your laptop and still not writing then time isn't the problem, the internet is. I use an internet blocking app. I didn't think I needed it as I'm pretty disciplined, but after doing the free trial I was surprised by how often the app showed I went online.

We can all justify our internet use by saying we need it for research, networking or socialising. But if this really is the case, you can make a little list of the things you need to look up (make this list on paper – not your phone) and check it all in one go at the end of the writing session.

I can personally resist doom-scrolling the news, other people showing off on Twitter and dancing cats on TikTok – but I absolutely cannot resist a bit of K-pop. It's the number one drain of my time. Do I have an imminent deadline for my next novel? Yes. Did I just spend twenty minutes watching a video titled 'Why you love Min Yoon-gi'? Also yes.

None of us are immune from these distractions – and it's not because we don't value our writing time, it's because the internet is bloody amazing. So switch it off. Work somewhere with no WiFi or if you can afford it, pay for an internet blocking app. I'd also suggest you keep your phone out of reach too.

§

Giving up

We've all been there. From the person who has just started and hasn't shown their writing to a soul, to the bestselling, award-winning author on a deadline. Sometimes the words don't come and you think: *Why the hell am I doing this when I could be watching videos of Min Yoon-gi on YouTube?*

Writing is hard. It's an odd, solitary hobby that most people don't understand. And when you feel like it's a waste of your time, or you're not good at it, or you don't know why you're doing it, then the ideas and words definitely won't find you.

So how to get out of these moods? Basically: sulk for a bit, moan to someone, eat something nice, take a sad walk. But after doing these things, you simply need to get over yourself. If you love writing and want to write you've got to keep going. You're the only person in the world who can tell whatever story it is you want to tell. Seriously. You're the only one. Your experience and world view are completely unique and the stories in your head can only be shared if you get them down on paper.

So I'll say it again: get over yourself.

Small wins

There's no end point in writing. Like most things in life the goalposts are constantly changing. You might think you'll celebrate when you finish a project, only to then want to get an agent, only to then want that publishing contract, only to then want that number one bestseller, only to then want that Hollywood film option . . . It's endless. So stop. Celebrate every win and let them inspire you to carry on. Whether it's getting that flash fiction piece polished to perfection or getting longlisted for a competition or even just being brave enough to admit to someone that you like to write – these things should be celebrated and enjoyed, because it's tough and every page is an achievement.

So go and write. Enjoy it, celebrate it and be inspired to do it all over again, because that is the process.

Origami

SAFA MARYAM

Tools needed:

Pen
Patience
You

Instructions:

1. Neatly unfurl to reveal
   the sharp corners of you
   that once hid folded over.

2. Smooth out creases
   storing the frowns
   of a life-long anger
   yet to be resolved.

3. Empty the paper pockets
   holding this week's despair
   that had nowhere
   to be put down until now.

4. Lift the central symmetrical flaps
   protecting the hope
   that insists on persisting
   despite it all.

5. Spread the paper flat,
   exposing a canvas
   free from the judgement
   of eyes not your own.

6. You now have the surface and space
   to reflect the waves
   of every colourful emotion
   seeking to be felt.

7. When finished and content,
   refold to be reborn
   as you find sense and meaning
   through each unfolding and feeling.

Baby

CHARLIE ROSE EVANS

My most recently abandoned protagonist is not taking her cue to leave. I am ice skating around the potential for conflict, gathering our dirty laundry into a pile, shredding final novel drafts into confetti to feed to the recycling bin. When I return from the office, I find her moping at the kitchen table, scooping out the ruby flesh of a grapefruit with a spoon. She has been filling the hours by reading about the antidepressant qualities of fruit, and gives me the same list every time I do the weekly shop: *Grapefruit x 10 (ORGANIC IF POSSIBLE!!!)*

Microsoft Word has settled into heavy-lidded hibernation. My laptop now exists for completing ten-minute surveys for 30p and caring for my Sims 4 household: Mum and Dad; two sets of twin toddlers; a poodle and cat. I love chaos when it's not my own. She sulks and slams doors when the loading screen pops up.

I have never felt this before: this sensation of the other person wanting to be with me more than I want to be with them. Sometimes I revel in it. I wear jewellery and paint my nails raspberry pink. Other times I am suffocated and can't tell which is my smell and which is hers. She helps herself to my repeat prescription, Jaffa Cakes and toothbrush.

We go to sleep on arguments, but it's usually forgotten about by morning. While I am out, she lies on her belly on the sofa and dissects my character studies, carving out the parts of her family that I have overlooked. It irks me. She is implying I didn't work hard enough.

I'm barely through the front door when she ambushes me.

'I need to know what happens to the baby,' she says, her lines so well-rehearsed and desperate. I order us a takeaway as a distraction and make a show of taking two paracetamols for a feigned migraine. Afterwards, when we lie in front of the TV, bloated and greasy and speckled in prawn cracker crumbs, I list her flaws on the back of a receipt. She dips cold chips into a pot of congealed curry sauce while I write. Our shared playlist rattles through my broken speakers. I run out of space, scrunch up the receipt and throw it, missing the bin. I am too bloated to walk over and pick it up. If I hadn't just given up trying to be the type of person who writes lists, it would go on my list of things to do tomorrow.

Sometimes I tell her the alternate endings. It makes her eyes light up so I keep going, coaxing the validation out. It spreads like a rash across my shoulders, warm and hungry to be itched. But the itch is incessant and impossible. There are half-moon nail imprints across my skin and the itch still won't be soothed, won't be reasoned with or rocked to sleep.

'And the baby?' she pleads one night, always ruining things.

My eyes scan the room in search of the green glow of the emergency exit. It is nowhere to be seen and the walls are caving in.

I snap. 'It's left open on purpose, I'm not writing that part.'

'But you're not writing any of it.' Her bottom lip wobbles. She holds her hot water bottle in the crook of her arm, then against her chest.

Her baths leave the flat sweaty and damp. I almost topple to my death, balancing on the closed toilet lid to paint over the mould contaminating the ceiling. I wonder what she would do without me. What I will do without her. We alternate roles: teenage daughter and mother, although we are the same age. I ask her to stop wiping up spilt milk with a clean tea towel, to start cleaning the tea towels, to stop spilling the milk. 'Come back soon,' she says, when I go out past six. Her abandonment issues are swelling like infected boils, ready to erupt. I want to pop them.

But then my heart softens at the most mundane times; when I am watering the office plants or waiting at bus stops – and I feel I can't blame her for how she gets under my skin. It is no wonder, when I have blood-let my flaws into her. All of my guilt. All of my messy, reactive, anti-social self-sabotage. We fly off the handle together, we blame, we bitch, we manifest disaster. We cry at the drop of a hat.

I think she might have found the receipt when she was pretending to vacuum. I think she scanned through the front first: spaghetti hoops, pink sprinkle donuts, oranges, grapefruits, bleach. Then she turned it over in her palm, and read what I wrote on the back in looping, smudged biro: *Not quite the right fit; not bowled over; tough current market; near miss this time; due to the sheer volume of submissions we receive we cannot offer individual feedback (so please jump to your own conclusions); your granny might have quite liked it when she was spell-checking, but it's not good enough for someone who doesn't know you, doesn't love you.*

I can hear her leaving: packing a bag, the fridge door groaning as she takes her grapefruits out and loads them into her coat pockets, lifting up the recycling, carrying it out.

§

In the evening, I counteract the newfound silence with a self-induced Sims hypnosis. When the poodle dies, I book the adults a day of compassionate leave from their jobs. They process the grief by trying for a baby. The baby looks just like her mother. The baby outgrows her, leaves her, builds an apple-selling business empire in her back garden. The baby sometimes thinks of her, and sometimes does not.

Application to Become a Writer

EMILY TUCKER

Position: Writer
Hours: variable,
frequent night shifts,
unpaid overtime
Holiday: n/a
Salary: ...

Please list below
the experiences and qualifications
that make you
the strongest candidate for this role.

Right,
where to start?
I've got a degree in English . . .

I've always loved to read
I sometimes wrote reviews
of moisturiser for
the student newspaper
But –
this isn't quite it.
Let me start over.

I was in a Pret
the other day and I remembered
the exact moment
that I chose one of my best friends.
I realised that I wanted
to keep him forever
over a can of that
sickly, half fizzy
yoga bunny drink.

Not long ago I heard a song
in a pub
about the Cemetery Gates.
That one by The Smiths.

I was sixteen again,
drinking shoplifted wine
and skipping tipsily
right into my first
heartbreak.

I was in the back of an Uber
somewhere near Arsenal
when I saw the kids waiting
by a Ladbrokes
and I thought
of my grandad,
the dead one
how we had to get to the pub
before the racing
to see him.
We were bad luck,
you see.

And I don't know if
you will have done,
But
did you ever notice
that when you find out
your boyfriend's
been cheating on you,
it feels like your stomach
will actually fall out of your body
and smack onto the floor?

And did you ever get hit?
By somebody you thought
loved you?

There's a strange magic
a sort of ridiculous fog
or a mist
straight afterwards
where you want to laugh
because
you don't think it actually
could have happened
to you.

The only time
I'm able to really
understand the way
I've clawed through
nearly three decades in this strange
little life
is when I put things down
into lines in an
untitled word document.

I don't know if
I'm sending out words
from myself to the
kids by the bookies.
Or if I'm trying to scrawl
I WAS HERE
somewhere into the walls.
Either way,
please just don't
make me stop.

In conclusion:
Yes,
there will be candidates with
bigger, better words,
tighter pitches,
nicer notebooks
and
a deeper understanding of
whatever meter and flow,
and you know,
all that stuff is.

BUT
if there is a single person
who might read my words
and know that
I've felt their awkward joys
and worried about all
the same stupid shite
that they may have,
you have no choice but
to give me this job.

I look forward to hearing
back from you in due course.

How to be a Writer

Call yourself a writer right now.

Do you write? Then call yourself a writer. What emotions do you feel when you tell people you're a writer? Is it difficult? Why? Get curious, but keep telling everyone. Practise on the taxi driver, the guy in the corner shop, your cat. If someone asks you what you've had published, tell them what you're working on instead. Never apologise or mumble into your sleeve if you haven't yet been published. Celebrate that you're writing, despite the inner critic, despite your fears, despite what others think. Own it. Shout about it.

You don't need a quill.

Write on your phone, on the train, anywhere. When I first started writing, I used some of my PhD funding to travel to Paris. I bought a black Moleskine notebook and I sat in all the cafés. I even wore a beret. No part of this performance improved any aspect of my writing. (I looked dead cute in that beret though.) Now I buy my notebooks from Wilkos. So just write and don't worry about how you get the words down.

Feed your head and feed your heart.

Nurture yourself with all kinds of art. Read widely. Be curious about what you like and what you don't. What do you connect with? What excites you? Develop trust in your own taste. Visit galleries and museums, take yourself away for trips (they don't have to be fancy). Relish and celebrate your obsessions. What thrills you? Porcelain Poirot ornaments? Then write about them. Don't worry about what others will think. The best writing is born from passion, not from trying to impress. Share your passions and you will find your people.

CHAPTER 2

Finding your Voice

I Said What I Said

MARIANNE TATEPO

You are whole.

Yet one day, you wake up next to a man who utters the words 'strong personality' as he speaks and you freeze.

'And I've been thinking...'

You are open to a confession. But this is about you: 'You are confident... in a way that makes me feel not so...'

Your breath catches.

'I do like women who are more fiery than me. And, I've been wondering if...'

Could it be?

'If this were to really become serious – which, I'm not saying this isn't – but, um. Actually, I've been wondering if maybe you might be too fiery for me?'

For all the tampered fire in your belly, another ending.

Goosebumps besiege you. Instants before, you were soft as he caressed your arm like so. You hang on to his every word and nearly let them mould you, as if your body were made of clay. His limbs rest on yours, heavy like a cloud in a rainstorm. He could break you right now.

Strong personality. (See also: *intimidating; argumentative; outspoken, for women, especially the darker ones. In case of a man, try: self-assured, inspiring, assertive. My guy!*) You want to poke that term around, to appraise it like a beached jellyfish for, given the chance, the wrong kind can sting you proper.

§

A few weeks later, you go to a party and meet a pair just like he and you – the four of you chew the fat in the moonlight until public transport comes to a halt. You become fast friends with the woman and the two of you begin to spend the weekends together: ice skating, roller blading, trading stories and making new friends. Eventually you relay this story to her: '…And then, he said that I have a strong personality; apparently he likes fiery women but I'm too fiery.' You wince. She rolls her eyes in solidarity, then smiles and says: 'But, that's why I like being your friend, though. You know who you are.'

You ask yourself: how can the attributes that the women in your life often praise you for become blunt weapons in the hands and mouths of men? How can your penchant for self-expression – the disposition that fuels your work life – become a signifier of inadequacy in your intimate one? How could it be that the men in – and soon enough, out of – your life find themselves bristling and flustered in this manner, their interest and care inversely proportional to the mindset that informs your intellect, your ease of being, your sense of peace, your sense of self?

§

This writer has sat in classrooms and libraries and read the books we were all told to, but in between those pages were galaxies missing.

Real people were often nowhere to be seen – the brazen Black boy who seeks tenderness. The queer Black girl who lusts and gets what she wants. The interactions that belied subtle grudges or ardent desires were often smoothed over. Women with unwavering wants were punished and jilted; Black women and enbies of this description had it the worst. Coming of age, my naturally curious nature was initially celebrated but gradually reviled, pathologised.

And so, what follows is what one writer wishes they'd been told when stepping into the world of reading, the world of writing – if not into the world altogether! It is for you – 'you' being a past version of myself, or maybe a curious onlooker leafing through the pages of this book, looking for reflections or refractions. These are the things one writer has learned over the years, which have guided their general approach to self-expression – writing, yes, but also talking. Because this writer's truth is that the way in which one listens and talks in the real world is what most informs the way one writes imagined ones. The writer's wilful disposition to notice what is around her, to question what she sees and is told, to say what she means and mean what she says, has done more for her than years of immersion into the codes of literary life. Below are the things which, given the chance, this writer would do all over again with the knowledge she'd write better for it.

If your enquiring nature has ever been pathologised, this is for you. If your love of long discussions that lead to an exchange of viewpoints ever begat the word 'intense', this is for you. If someone you've loved or wanted has ever laughed at your desire to create, to make, to write, this is also for you. If you're still trying to find your voice, this too is for you. If you just need a reminder about all that you can do – it's all for you. It is but one writer's story, but sometimes all it takes to start a revolution is a single story.

§

When you are six years old, your school puts out a callout for a play. It is around the time that some people around you – those who can determine your livelihood, and sometimes even those who care about you – start trying to give you roles that you do not want. They give you space, but it is not always the space you'd like to have.

But you don't know this yet, and so you volunteer. Not just that, you go for the only part that requires a functional outfit, and turn up in a two-piece houndstooth suit from Paris with red lapels and a hat like in *Madeline*. It does not matter that you are six years old. Somehow, you own a goddamn suit and orate in a manner that befits your part of president, Obamaesque save for the anachronism of it all, equal parts Mich and Barry. You are a gap-toothed joyous child whose mother often has to shush her for gormlessly repeating fragments of overheard hushed conversations in public.

Around this time, you visit your parents' native Cameroon and decide that one day you want to be its president. Never mind that it is only on its second ruler in its thirty-plus year history. You know little other than the fact that you want to absorb all the facts you can and give everyone a voice and a better life.

Questioning things gives you purpose, and sometimes you also have something to say, and people sometimes even listen. Of course, the only reason why you notice people listening is that it's a corrective for all the times when it feels like they don't – who are you anyway? For all the shushing, elbows like nettles, you sit at the dinner table with your elders and on occasion interject while they talk about the topic of the day, be that football, music or religion.

Wednesdays are half days at school. When you come home, the TV is showing the French Senate. In this regal assembly, pompous men who resemble birds of prey proselytise the nation as they lament the perils of migration and the erosion of traditional values (by which they think 'western civilisation', by which they really mean, whiteness). Every night, the news comes on right after *The Simpsons*, sometimes interrupting it. You have a version of your own, a children's news edit. You stare at the 4:3 screen for hours, and often spend the evenings scribbling in notebooks, concocting stories of secret dragons and orphans. You love the world, you love nature, you love stories – but you won't tell anybody. Your notebooks are adorned with heart-shaped padlocks and you hide the key in cryptic vaults, far away from the prying eyes of siblings.

In years to come, your family starts to see something in you that you don't. To them your natural disposition is sullen or quiet; sulky and standoffish. You start to question yourself, and the world. Somewhere in all that searching, the seed of writing sprouts.

§

You tell yourself to be good. Though on a couple of occasions, you find yourself glued to the floor, the incomparable ringing noise that echoes long after someone's palms and knuckles make one with the outline of your face. Sometimes you regret standing up for yourself so vocally after this person disrespected you, knowing full well there is no lesson learned here, and they will do it again. But if you hadn't, who would have? Who would have stood up for the little girl in the room the adults have decided doesn't look enough like a child to warrant protection? When you've caught enough punches and your hair has been pulled out real good and they are taunting you, you might mutter an apology. A sorry for your impudence; for your existence. You whisper it to yourself as they walk away and leave you lying on the side of a deserted thoroughfare. You are fourteen years old.

Was it worth it, opening that big mouth of yours?

§

But you learn to fight. Well, in your own way. You start to pick your battles.

At 16, you sign up for and secure a spot on the school's debating team. It's a posh school, and the format is like Model United Nations, except that with it being in Brussels, your hometown, the European Parliament trumps the UN! You enjoy the thrill of considering ideas that you would never adopt as your own. Around this time, you are studying the basic tenets of philosophy and learn about rhetorical arguments, their formulas like the algebra you so abhor. For months, you go to a hollowed-out classroom every Tuesday after school and, with a dozen others, look at arguments to put forward ahead of the Model European Parliament three-day assembly. Although in almost every aspect of your life, centrism is something to shirk, you find yourself assigned the role of chairperson for the European People's Party, on behalf of the UK, and are in charge of running the agriculture and fisheries council.

Amidst the jargon of debating, a stirring begins inside you. This is the year when you start pulling together a portfolio of writing. Focused on your studies now, you have singled out five universities to apply to. Your favourite course demands a portfolio submission. Lately, giving in to teenage erudition, you have been obsessed with the dystopias of Orwell and Burgess. You compose a dystopia of your own: an imagined world in which whiteness is forced upon anyone of colour who lives in the Western world. For range, you also compose alliterative poetry (this is your Baudelairian phase). The collection of some 40-odd pages of prose and poems earns you a place on a bachelor's degree in literature and creative writing. But you're not quite sure. Unlike London, it's in a town you've never been to, and you have no idea how you're supposed to pay two £2,000 instalments for accommodation. At least in London, there's a steady influx of casual jobs.

Not long before this time, you've gotten seriously into music. At least once a month, you have a routine consisting of the following: spending ten euros on gig tickets (all gathered from recycling used bottles); five euros of pocket money on an issue of NME and popping by Waterstones for paperbacks' sake. In years to come, a faded price stamp indicates that you once paid nearly twelve euros for an eight quid paperback of *The Catcher in the Rye*. All these extracurriculars are part of the plan: you want to lean into the plurality of language, debating others in English and French. You want to boost your CV for UCAS, and, eventually, you would like to leave this place – at least by travelling first. This much you know: there are worlds outside the city, but also within you. You set your sights on London a couple of years prior.

After a successful first debating stint, you put yourself forward again the following year, which is your final school year. Your teachers say something along the lines of, 'We don't allow students to participate more than the one time, it's really competitive'. You smile after successfully using your newly acquired debating skills to secure a second stint. This year, you fly to Spain and represent Malta as part of the Model European Council and your focus is transport and energy. You think of it as a debating club, but there is no winner at the end. The purpose of the exercise is a mere sharpening of the mind, exposure to different viewpoints and also the excuse of bunking off school for a few days to sit in the Benidorm rays. But this doesn't make you all take it any less seriously, sixteen-year-olds cosplaying as MPs and journalists.

One day, a girl from a rival school writes a piece about you where she takes a jab at your informal use of language during a session. Whether in character or otherwise, it's hard to say in hindsight, but you walk up to her after a session, brandishing the shabbily printed newspaper, slamming it on her desk in a manner akin to Paris Geller from Gilmore Girls.

'So, do you have anything else to add, beyond whatever it is you put in this article?' You level the accusation at her. She fumbles for excuses, breaking the fourth wall momentarily as she admits that she was just trying to write something interesting, but you stay in character, eventually getting a proper apology for that slander; proud that you've learned how to stand up for yourself. So what, if your mother gave you the name of a spontaneous and at-times thoughtless Austenian heroine and the French metonymy and mono-boob-flashing revolutionary symbol, Marianne?

Around this time, you learn what is worth fighting for.

§

At 18, you are years away from interrogating power.

You get close to someone, really close. He leans in all the way when you reveal you're studying literature and have tailored a big portion of your life around the written word. He loves to write, he says. He sometimes types out sonnets that he texts you via BBM. You coo; you cheer. You are in a writing workshop, you are writing songs. The workshop facilitates your first and perhaps last ever attempt at autofiction as you document the *Gossip Girl*-esque cast of characters you meet during your university days – their quirks and vices. Using a prompt given by your lecturer, you write about the experience of leaving home for the first time. It is clunky, it is trite. But it is something, and it is yours. Once you share a song with this boy you care about; all he does is laugh. You don't take it to heart, until you tell him about the project you'd like to start, the writing chronicling those precious years of your life. He mocks the very idea that you could ever see something through. In your time together, you never so much as pick up a pen. You spend a portion of your time together unable to enjoy the sound of music, forgetting the downward pull of sticky floors and the uplifting appeal of live music: your balm. All you can hear is his wicked cackle as you realise the pathetic smallness of you turning to him saying, 'Look at what I've made!' and you feel less like a child showing pasta art and more like an infant whose only way to express itself is cry.

§

Eventually, you begin to remember who the fuck it is you are. And who you are is someone who loves to think, to question, to write. To dance to music, to fill the air with lyrics from Arctic Monkeys, Metronomy, Animal Collective. You are someone who believes in the people around her, as well as herself. Who is unafraid to voice what she thinks, who is excited when exchanging theories, thoughts and comments about a piece of art. So where did you go, and when did 'girlfriend' become your Homeric epithet?

§

You have this long-held idea that the fatal flaw of the gender binary is that when most men feel the weight of failure or rejection, they externalise it. They look for someone else to enact their anger and sense of smallness on. Conversely, you believe that when most women feel that they have been rejected or failed, they often internalise that shame, blaming themselves for that pervasive not-good-enough-ness or too-much-ness that so many of us are taught to live with. And more often than not, those two types of people find one another, as you both did.

When you meet his mother, she confesses that she is surprised he went on to do a traditional vocational degree when his true love was always literature. You glare in his direction as he sips and in that moment you are the poster child of the idiom 'if looks could kill'.

When you finally break up, you wish you could tell him – among the countless reasons why – that it's less about leaving him, more about running back towards yourself.

Within a year, you have filled four notebooks.

You start to notice what you are good at. Because you are good, at a few things, however mundane. And writing is just scaffolding

– there are parts to this craft that you can pick up over time. This pride at knowing you can master at least one thing in life will save you. You start to look at the things that you'd like to, at least, be mediocre at. And then you get started.

§

You are 23 years old and working a day job that has you scanning through Excel spreadsheets all day and facilitating other people's creativity as you predict the millions due to pour into company accounts that year. You are an organiser and a coordinator and a problem solver – for everyone but yourself. You are good at helping the people around you figure out what they want out of life, and you help them to do it. But your heart's not in it. What is it you want? What is it you really want?

You have been out of academia for a while and forgotten what it is really like to read for pleasure. At lunch, you learn to go on breaks to read and eat – *A Little Life*, *Essays on Love*. You walk around heaps of vertiginous concrete and realise what you have known all along, since you were a child. You were seven years old and your sister gifted you what you now reckon was *Fantastic Mr Fox*. You furrowed away then, disappearing for the rest of Christmas Eve to read. You want to feel that transcendent feeling again, and again, and again.

At 26, you have been training and interning and working in the literary world for a couple of years, when you finally land your first serious editorial job. The hours of spreadsheets, and planning and coordinating and organising finally make sense. You can have all of this rolled into one. You can work with people who have a creative mind in a creative way. You can spend hours lost in thought with ideas that hundreds of thousands of people will carry with them through the years. Your work has purpose. You are your intellectual self again.

§

You are 28. You started a new job a few weeks ago and now here you are on your sofa, idly biding your time in lockdown. They call it 'furlough' and it won't make sense to anyone who wasn't there at the time. It is indefinite time off with some degree of assurance in the form of income but no degree of certainty in the form of an end date. More importantly, it is devoid of daily responsibilities, focus, purpose.

You are in a liminal space between vacation and redundancy. Between a post-racial and white supremacist society. Between sickness and health. In late May of that year, an African American man is murdered by the police in cold blood; his name is George Floyd. A couple of days later, you watch the whole of London take to the streets to protest, alone at home with COVID. You think about communion, about community, about Blackness, about what freedom of expression really means to you.

While working isn't, volunteering is an option. So, you set up a community for Black agents and editors in UK publishing, and call it BAE. You love an acronym. In the before times, work was also a space to socialise, and now it's a sofa. It was a place to think and exchange ideas, and now it's a sofa. It was an actual place, and now it literally is just a sofa! During the few months you spend on it, you redefine community, and create a group that informs conversations around race, class, privilege and prejudice in your industry.

You are now working as a fully fledged acquiring editor, too aware of the dearth of others like you – so part of BAE becomes about mentoring the next generation, so that they can be part of shaping the literary landscape, too. For the first time, you feel like you have found your calling: the job of editor literally rewards you for both being able to think ideas through to death while at the same time having the confidence to know when to say 'enough', thanks to time constraints of printing. It empowers you to seek out bold voices, to nurture them, and to use your own to elevate them. You edit and publish books on food and drink, parenting, neuroscience, interior design, sexual violence, journalling, existentialism.

Here, you learn a lot about the writer. The writer uses the second person to pretend to be someone else. The writer asserts their boundaries, through the medium of the page. The writer questions decisions. The writer challenges. The writer crafts cryptic sentences which sometimes only they can decipher fully. The writer avoids trauma porn. The writer is vulnerable but not intimate. The writer bears witness but does not confess. The writer borrows from life but also lives in it, fully. The writer is argumentative, assertive and bold. And, sometimes, the writer has a strong personality, too. More than ever, you want to be a writer, you love being a writer.

§

You are pushing 30 – ushering in the new decade feels like finally arriving at a party you had warily schlepped to, anxious about running late. You are asked to write a piece about the importance of finding your voice, of telling your story. Well, what do you know about that now? What have you learned?

§

Finding our voice is often intimately linked to figuring out what modes of expression we will be rewarded for (by society, family, friends, lovers, institutions); or at least those that won't punish us. What parts of our psyche and thinking would we really bare if we didn't fear intellectual stigmatisation, or mockery? And which parts would we keep to ourselves?

Around the world, for most women, there is a certain cultural expectation that to be kind is to be quiet, to be respectable is to acquiesce. In other words, to preserve the status quo. But what exciting writing has ever happened through mere acquiescence about the way things are? No thought-provoking writing has been born out of a deep desire to appease, to fit in. Disruption for its own sake, mere contrarianism, is never the goal: this writer cares about people, and how words affect them (and vice versa). But more than anything else, this writer cares about truth – about doing what is good (for the story, for one's sense of transparency and accountability), even if it occasionally means saying something that feels less so. This writer believes in the act of writing as a form of truth, of bearing witness to the fact we exist – that you exist. That we are both here now, writer and reader, reflecting or disagreeing – or in the best of cases, somewhere in between.

And sometimes just to exist and acknowledge that we exist – that we have made it this far, that we are still here, bearing witness, page by page, archiving and living life word by word and question by question – is to be whole; is everything.

Peaches and Jazz

KATJA KNEŽEVIĆ

I listen to a lesson on writing
on how to find one's voice, one's
'persona', the poet calls it, before

proclaiming his is decidedly
non-autobiographical.
he sits in a leather armchair

glasses perched on the tip of his nose,
a knowing smile flickers across the room.
he seldom looks at his past and how

I envy that, his ability to sketch out
and stretch out the now, unattached
to past nows,

because I am unable to hold
on to just one string, before I know it,
it weaves itself out of my hands

and into others; they rush to each other
like long-separated family members.
still I try: look down on the paper then up

out the window for inspiration.
but the hands of the student next to me
look like my late grandmother's, and

my persona runs off the stage
I had prepared – with a punch to the stomach
I am thrust back. I am four again

in the soldiers' van with my grandma.
where are we going and where is Mom?
Tears mix with vomit,

hands cover my ears
I know nothing; there is only needing
to be elsewhere, elsewho:

someone who is listening to jazz
reading a slow sonnet
sitting in a brown leather armchair
a bowl of peaches on a coffee table.

What is this impossibility?
What would a four-year-old know
about peaches and jazz?

This isn't her memory
it's the now-me, shoving the image
in the place of her yearning

it is what she needs this time, every time
it's a different trick, I give her that
what I hold at the moment

Writing Not Bleeding

ELSPETH WILSON

It started with a notebook and the feeling that I needed to slice myself down the middle and wrench something book-shaped out. It began with my only friends close at hand being blank pages. It started with telling secrets to no one but myself yet feeling as if I was telling them to a million people. It started with the compulsion, the need, to translate what my body was feeling into language my mind could comprehend.

§

I was living in Dublin and didn't know anyone. I'd met a guy. I'd had an abortion. I'd traveled through some of the most beautiful scenery I'd ever seen in my life. I'd found that swimming in the sea helped me to live in my body. I had plenty to say but no one to say it to. All the friends I'd made in my new home had moved away, leaving me alone in the city – apart from the guy. He was busy doing his engineering degree, crafting useful things to be used by useful people. So, I thought I'd do the same. Or the opposite. I'm not sure.

Once I'd put pen to paper, it was like all the combined sorrows, all those small things that can add up to make living as a (disabled) woman seem impossible, had been brought back to life. I was hungry. I dug up every experience I could remember, every relationship I could dissect, every bad thing that had ever happened to me that I hadn't been able to talk about. Until now. All the trauma, all the wounds and blood, literal and otherwise, flowed out of me, uncontrolled. They were resurrected from wherever I'd buried them – except this time, I could control them. This time, I was channelling them out through my hand, not to excise but to rearrange them into something I could understand beyond feeling. Something that I could read back, ponder, think upon.

I wrote in the evenings, after long days at the office where I'd also sneak in writing on my lunch break, my hand itching with the need to process and tell. Then I'd slump on my bed exhausted from wringing out words from every spare moment. Sometimes I'd go for a walk to the Blessington Street Basin, my tiny local park, and just sit and stare at the moorhens on the pond, watching them swim round and round in circles through the tall rushes. It's hard work pouring yourself out, then poring over it. It's hard work thinking the only purpose, the only thing that your writing is good for, is to provide a therapist when you can't afford one, to try to find a modicum of sense in your most traumatic experiences, to live in hope that writing out your own pain will prevent someone else's.

I'd fall asleep, emptied. But in the morning, I'd always feel the need to find release all over again.

§

I'm not saying that the excavation and spilling of hurt and pain didn't help; it did. That sharing was like being fourteen years old at a sleepover again, when you confess all kinds of things under the cover of dark. That notebook with the silver hare on the blue cover was there when I needed it, when what soothed me most was being able to unspool myself on the page. And I was praised for all this introspection; I was told by writing tutors at evening classes and online workshops that this kind of self-examination would make my writing interesting and compelling and publishable.

But needs change. I moved away from the place where I knew no one and the guy stopped doing his engineering degree. He had more time for me, meaning I had less time for writing which made me feel guilty but not unhappy. At first, I felt bad for not putting my pain on the page but I didn't really have any more pain to give. In school and in writing workshops, I'd been told again and again about 'tortured geniuses' and artists suffering for their craft – almost always rich, white men who had other people to do their cooking and cleaning. I fell into the trap of thinking that I had nothing to share now that I was content. That I no longer harboured the kind of pain a writer needs. That maybe it was wrong for an artist to be happy at all.

§

The funny thing was that the page kept calling me back, despite me supposedly having little left for it. As I experienced more joy, tranquility and pleasure, there was more I wanted to scribble down, not less. I wanted to record those moments of relaxing into the arms of the person you love most in the world. Trying out a new, complicated recipe and seeing how it turns out compared to the glossy photos, or getting to the top of a hill, sweaty and breathless, to see a view that you've seen countless times and be moved by it all over again.

It took sharing a poem that I'd written in five minutes on my phone with a close friend to realise that I didn't have to take every bit of writing 'advice' to heart. I'd written about a visit to a local beach with my mum and all the different butterflies we'd seen, the way the grasses had tickled my bare legs and how the different versions of our past selves walked alongside us. My friend smiled – my words really connected with her – and I got watery-eyed in a happy way, shocked that someone could enjoy hearing about something I thought so simple, so mundane. I knew then that I could make space for joy in my writing and expand my creativity beyond any narrow confines.

§

During lockdown, when I was feeling overwhelmed or alone, I noticed birds or children playing outside and doggedly noted down small, interesting, eye-catching details. By putting words on the page, I made friends with my surroundings and survival turned slowly to existence, and then to actual living. This process transformed my understanding and experience of nature in domestic places – like houseplants, spiders, mice – which in term prompted me to write about biodiversity and climate crisis in different ways. I didn't set out intending to do that, but noticing everyday moments of hope around me allowed me to approach big and urgent topics in a way that I would never have discovered if I hadn't given myself the opportunity to start small, slowly and mindfully.

I took the long route to understanding that changing the world doesn't have to come from a place of hurt. Our writing doesn't even have to change the world; it can just change you, or your mood, or your father's thoughts on something and it will still have enacted an emotional reaction of some sort. Through these lockdown explorations and through sharing my words with others, I have found that writing which is relational, which reaches out beyond pages and headphones, and wraps itself around many different hearts often contains the hopeful, the happy, the joyous, and the tranquil.

It's a long way from the reasons I began writing but in some ways it feels like closing the loop. I started because I felt so angry and sad and lost about so many things in my life, in life in general and in the world, and I hoped that – even if only to a tiny extent – I could write a different future into existence. For writing to inspire change it has to present change as a possibility, a potential – the things that I have written that people have told me have moved them have often been pieces where I have drawn from a stubborn well of optimism that things have to get better and I have to contribute to it, in however small a way.

A writing tutor once told me that 'happiness writes white'. But my happiness has been every single colour of the rainbow. It has been a cool blue on the days where I breathe into my body and let myself feel places that I thought were cut off. It has been ketchup red when I have danced around my living room with abandon, singing completely tunelessly to lyrics I know by heart. It has been the palest of purples when stroking my elderly dog, who always had time for me, a lolloping gait and a soft pink tongue. It has been a soft, mossy green when I have finally, *finally* got prescribed the right medication to allow my body some rest. And it has been a gold so bright that it's hard to look at when I have reclaimed my pleasure, rewritten my own map, crossing out the claims others have made on my body.

§

These days, I think consciously about what I want to show people, and how, and I keep some of my most private writing just for me. Too many of us are expected to bleed our whole lives long. We are told that there is only a demand for a certain kind of story from people like us, and the ending is rarely a happy one. Of course, writing about trauma can be cathartic and important, both for writers and readers, but it can also be risky and potentially re-traumatising, especially if not done on the author's own terms.

And if we do tell our stories in the way that we are often funneled into, we get told that our stories are singular. That that's all we are good for. So if there's already one of us out there – against the odds – then that person who might share one characteristic with us but is otherwise a whole, complete different individual has cornered the market and no one else will want to read another disabled/neurodivergent/queer/insert here story.

There's a very specific kind of violence in society treating us a certain way and then limiting our art to lopping bits of ourselves off and offering them up for public consumption; in suggesting our personhood and our stories only amount to the lack of personhood which they manifested and afforded us in the first place.

Here's the thing. We don't have to bleed on the page. We can if we choose to but we don't have to. And if we do, we can keep it private or make it public or do whatever the hell we choose.

So bleed if you want to. I did for a long while and it felt good, did me good, for a time. Now, I'm gentle with myself when I press my sore points – I make time to look after myself and do all the other things that I love alongside writing. Instead of blood, I write with simple old ink.

Finding
your Voice

Don't put your bowtie on.

Don't strain for fancy or write how you think a writer 'should'. If you're starting out, it's a good idea to write in your internal voice, or as if you're talking to a good friend you can tell anything to. Be honest and authentic. This is what readers will respond to most.

Don't judge yourself.

The road to good writing is paved with crappy writing. There will come a point when your sentences snap into place, your characters sing and the whole business of writing is not quite as hard as it once was. This takes time. So give yourself this time without judgement. Self-compassion is so important, and so is allowing yourself the space to learn.

Be an authority.

There's nowhere to hide on the page. If you're tentative, the reader can tell a mile off. You have to state: *look, here, this is how the world is for me. This is how the world is for my characters.* It doesn't matter if you're the most anxious person in the world – writers are generally anxious people – but on the page you have to write with authority. *Sit. Listen to me.*

CHAPTER 3

Inner Critic

Where the Wild Things Are

KERRY RYAN

When I was growing up in Glasgow, positive reinforcement was not a popular concept. You were just as likely to be slagged off by your granny as the kids in your street. 'Getting a pounding', we called it. The understanding being that words could pound you as hard as fists. Shaming was the norm. Gentle parenting was certainly not the done thing. Children were meant to be frightened of their parents. How else would you learn to behave? And then there was school.

Over the years, I've noticed that the majority of published writers have something in common: a Miss Honey. I call her Miss Honey – that sweet teacher from *Matilda* – but it might be Mr Smith or Ms Kumar. Someone in a position of authority who, when the writer was young and their mind still a sponge, said: 'You're good at this. A writing life can be yours.' You'll spot these Miss Honeys in dedications, in acknowledgements, in Booker

Prize-winning speeches. 'Thank you, Miss Honey, for always believing in me.'

Miss Honeys were thin on the ground at my school. Plenty of Trunchbulls though, along with a good amount of alcoholics and predators. The school was closed and bulldozed a few years after I left to take A-levels at the local college. This was after the head-teacher looked down his nose at me and said: 'Someone like you will never go to university.' Be assured, this was not a misguided attempt at reverse psychology: it was pure malice.

Now and then, through the years, I've thought of that head-teacher. To be in charge of the learning and development – the futures – of hundreds of working-class pupils, many experiencing abject poverty, and take pleasure in saying such a thing to a beauti-ful, bright, eager-to-learn student. What bitterness he must have carried. What disappointments.

I met with similar men at college then university. Weak men in positions of power who took pleasure in instilling doubt, in questioning ability and worth. What did they wish to snuff out? Hope, ambition, the power to rise and soar way ahead. But wild-ness, I think, most of all. The free wild spirit inside.

As we know, the programming to be 'good' – polite, quiet, humble – begins when we are girls. From fairy tales onwards, we're taught how dangerous it is to have a voice, to boast, to be prideful, to be an 'attention whore'. Then, as adults, we watch women in the public eye – singers, actors, TV presenters, writers – hounded and vilified. As Siri Hustvedt writes, when a woman claims authority or is recognised as an authority by others, she risks punishment. Her authority is only tolerated if 'she shows communality, if she softens her knowledge with smiles, deferent, pleasing looks, or even better, gives lots of credit to others for her work or declares herself really, really lucky.' And often, this is not enough. Some women are still hounded. Some even lose their lives.

Sadly, what Hustvedt calls 'patriarchy's law enforcement units' are very often women. There is a website I won't name where, each evening, thousands of women log on – perhaps with a nice Rioja after kissing their kids goodnight – and gleefully tear other women to shreds. Their crime? To have a public profile. To claim some kind of authority as mothers, influencers, vloggers, chefs, actors. To not be humble enough or to be so humble it must be fake. They are always too much or not enough.

A novel is rejected and fear freezes us. A novel is accepted and the same thing happens. Success is as terrifying as failure because, as we've witnessed, women in the public eye are so often punished for having a voice. When we start to write, the inner critic senses the potential for social shame, and it sirens into red alert. By constantly pointing out that we're not good enough, the inner critic hopes to avoid tribal shame by creating enough discomfort and fear of being rejected to either motivate us to do more, to be perfect, or to avoid doing anything at all. We can go on marches, sign petitions, read a thousand books on taking up space yet the programming to stay 'safe' in the shadows can run at a deep, unconscious level, preventing us from making authentic art and sharing our unique view of the world.

For years, I hid. I told myself I was learning my craft, which I was, yes, but I was also hiding. From success. From failure. Every so often, I'd emerge from my cave and share a piece of writing I'd been secretly working on. *Is this any good?* I would ask. *Is it worthwhile?* But all along, I was actually asking: *Am I any good? Am I worthwhile?*

I no longer ask these kinds of questions. Or, not often. Only now and then when the moon is full. But I did. Oh, I did. My inner critic was a monster. A stalking night creature, panther-black, beautiful yet terrible and so powerful. It had my mind clamped between its jaws for years; canines skewering the soft grey meat of my brain. I couldn't free myself, no matter how hard I fought.

§

In Maurice Sendak's *Where the Wild Things Are*, a little boy, Max, puts on his wolf suit and runs around his house causing havoc. His mother calls him Wild Thing and sends him to bed without his supper after Max threatens to eat her up. But that night a forest grows in Max's room and an ocean rushes by with a boat to take him to the place where the wild things are. Max escapes his shame at being 'bad' by using his imagination to travel the realm of the unconscious, the realm of the imagination. But in order to play and dance and sing freely, first Max has to look his monsters – the wild things – in the eye. In this way he tames them and becomes the King of all Wild Things.

Sendak was interested in how we survive our childhoods and how we can thrive as adults. For Sendak, art is always the answer. There is catharsis through the creation of story and image but in order to experience that catharsis we have to reign over our inner monsters. We do this not by fleeing or fighting in fear, but by standing firm and strong and looking those stalking night creatures square in the face. Then they are tamed and we are free to sing and dance and play on the page. Free to be wild.

In Ursula K. Le Guin's *A Wizard of Earthsea*, Ged uses his magic, his brilliant talent, to show off, for ego's sake, for validation and applause because he is poor and insecure. His actions bring a terrible shadow into the world. The shadow hampers his friendships and his prospects. His magic is weakened. He can't become who he should be. He fights this wild shadow to no avail and then he runs from it. He tries to discover the creature's true name because in Earthsea to know a thing or person's true name is to master it. But he's at a loss. Finally, he stops running. He travels to the ends of the earth and meets this shadow face to face. He speaks its true name which is his own name: *Ged*. He embraces his shadow and by embracing it, he masters it and is free to make magic. He is free to create.

Jung called this process of embracing our shadow and coming into psychological wholeness *individuation* and Le Guin, like Sendak, was heavily influenced by Jung. Individuation is when we stop running from all the wild monsters we repress – envy, fear, shame – and instead we turn towards them with compassion and curiosity. Our old monsters – our programming from the past, from culture and society – no longer stand between us and the really wild, juicy creativity in the depths of our unconscious. Our fear of shame, of failure no longer keeps us small and trapped in the jaws of the inner critic. As Le Guin wrote: 'The shadow stands on the threshold. We can let it bar the way to the creative depths of the unconscious, or we can let it lead us to those depths.'

Le Guin had been writing for over twenty years and had five novels and a book of poetry rejected before the award-winning *A Wizard of Earthsea* was published. It's not difficult to see the parallels between Ged's hero's journey – embracing his dark shadow in order to create true magic – and Le Guin's own creative journey.

If we're going to face our shadow, compassion is a must. Yet to love our flawed human selves unconditionally and ignore the unreachable standards our inner critic has set can feel like an impossible task. Even if we've had a Miss Honey, a supportive someone or several supportive someones, adverse childhood experiences or being othered because of our sexuality, race, age, gender, disabilities can create an inner critic so vicious that it drowns out our compassionate inner voice. I remember in my early twenties reading Derek Walcott's poem: 'Love After Love'. The poem counsels that you should give back your heart to the stranger who has loved you all of your life. Who was this stranger, I wondered? A sister? Another lover? That there could be a wise compassionate mentor – a Miss Honey – inside all of us was such an alien concept that it took time for the poem's meaning to click and a lot longer before I practiced the self-love it preached. Now I do. Every single day.

Being a Miss Honey for others helps too. I am the teacher I never had. 'You can do it. I believe in you,' I tell my students but I am telling myself too. By helping others rewrite their internal narrative, we learn how to rewrite our own. Ask any therapist.

§

Yesterday began with my son and I singing silly songs in bed. After I had taken him to school, I came home and brewed my favourite tea in the blue polka-dot teapot I bought in Paris. I sat in a patch of sunlight on my yellow sofa and did my daily tarot reading. Then I scrawled out my morning pages upstairs in my writing room – a dream of a room, a glass box made of light with views of the hills and the rolling sea. I sat at my desk for a few hours and I played. I dreamed up a short story and a poem, trusting my unconscious to guide me, and I kept going even when my inner critic started growling. After a while, my back ached, so I went downstairs with my laptop and wrapped myself in my duvet and did some freelance proofreading while listening to the radio. Then I had a chat on Zoom with one of my very first students. She's about to run my courses in her hometown and I'm so pleased.

After I closed my laptop, it was school pick-up and dog walking and dinner and karate outfits and domestic life with all its wonders and despair. In the late evening, my son read my old copy of *Charlie and the Chocolate Factory* while I zoomed with my writing group. I love those women: Miss Honeys, queens of the wild, women who know what strength it takes to meet your monsters. We shared writing and supported each other and laughed a lot. Finally, it was my son's bedtime. Soon he'll be too big for our nighttime routine of hugs and songs, so I laid down beside him as his moon and stars mobile twisted and turned in a mystery breeze, and I savoured it all.

Lights out and I took a cup of herbal tea to bed with a book – a novel so powerful that I was reminded all over again of why I love literature. And in the morning, this morning before I edited these words for you, I found a surprise package at the front door. My student's new novel – sent as if she knew I was writing this essay because inside was was a note: 'Thank you for always believing in me.'

If I'd listened to the inner critic, this span of twenty-four hours would have been all failure. What would my inner monster have found wanting? All of it. The sentences I wrote; how slow I was; how old I am; my dialogue; my description. Then there would be my parenting, my teaching, my admin skills. This day – the kind I dreamed of when I was a wee lassie devouring books in the Carnegie library – would have had all the colour drained from it. Greyed to ash because someone somewhere was writing more fluently, winning more prizes, getting more credits. There is always a better someone somewhere. Our ideal writer.

The ideal writer lurks in our psyche, tucked away beyond the reach of rational thought. We don't notice when our inner critic – always on shame patrol – compares us to this figment of our imagination. Our ideal writer might be a Frankenstein's monster of all the writers we admire or perhaps it's a composite of the writers others admire and applaud. Whoever it is, the inner critic compares and contrasts and finds us wanting. *This isn't a sentence Zadie Smith would write. This isn't a plot a bestselling literary novelist would use.* We are published yes, but not by Penguin. *Must try harder. Must do better. Must not write the fun story about the Baba Yaga and instead write the kind of story Granta will publish.* Or: must hide away, perfecting, perfecting, until our writing is so polished that editors faint at the sight of our sentences. *Must. Do. Better.* And on the whip cracks. So many precious moments lost to compare and contrast.

In order to exorcise the ideal writer and shrink the inner critic, we don't lose our ambition or our drive but we do examine our creative intentions and what might lie in the shadow of our psyche. What is it exactly that terrifies us so much? Where do these fears come from? Why do we write? To reach little girls in the Carnegie library in a post-industrial Scottish town who need a friend, who need respite, who need to be shown that other lives are possible? For the joy of connecting and learning our craft? Or is it about approval and validation? *Am I any good? Am I worthwhile?*

Humans in general aren't big fans of uncertainty and the writing life is all uncertainty. If we hook our self-worth onto such a subjective medium and live and die by what others determine is success or failure then we're screwed. The uncertainty of the writing life will be too much to bear because there is too much at stake.

There was a time when I'd scent failure and head straight back to my cave, where instead of writing, I'd search for jobs in the civil service with solid pensions. My attitude is different now. I move towards uncertainty. When the inner critic gets loud, instead of fighting, fleeing or hanging defeated in the monster's jaws, I move towards it. I embrace my shadow. Of course what helps is that I have my own internal Miss Honey now, always encouraging, always loving no matter what. The *no matter what* is key. In this way I reign supreme over weak men and monsters.

Compassion is essential, yes, but anger helps too. Anger that women spend years hiding in their own lives. Anger that women are frightened, shamed and silenced. Anger that all over the world women are dying when they speak their truth. Having a voice is a radical act in a society that would prefer you voiceless. Anger as well as compassion can help break your silence. 'Seize attention,' the brilliant activist Mona Eltahawy writes in *The Seven Necessary Sins For Women and Girls*. 'There is revolutionary power in saying *I count*.'

Until I have no days left, this is how I shall spend them: writing, reading, going where the wild things are and supporting others to do the same. Loving my heart and my free wild spirit. Dreaming with my eyes wide open. Seizing attention and saying *I count*. Every single day. I hope you do too.

Thorns Start Out as Branches

• Fiction •

CHARLOTTE TURNBULL

I n March, a week after Ruth's debut novel published in paperback, the hawthorn tree at the highest point of her garden was pulled out by a digger.

She had initially asked a local gardener to do it.

'She's gert old,' he said. 'Prune 'er back. She'll be no trouble.'

'No,' Ruth said. 'My new writing shed is going—' She pointed straight into the bunched fist of branches, the spot that looked onto the long tongue of the moor.

The man shook his head, and glanced behind him. 'Put it somewhere else. Or you'll have trouble wi' thee piskies.'

Ruth laughed, then frowned. 'No. This is the view. I need the inspiration – the focus of nature.'

Her mother had flinched when Ruth told her about the shed. 'Oh god,' she said, putting a hand either side of her face and lowering her voice, 'you're not getting one of those fake shepherd's huts, are you?'

Ruth was affronted. 'Of course not. It's a completely ordinary shed. Apart from the skylights. And the bi-folding French doors.' Ruth hoped her mother would understand when she saw it.

'Well,' said her mother. 'Hide yourself out of sight, at the bottom of the garden. Otherwise people might ask tricky questions about what you're doing in there.'

When it became clear that the gardener would not help her with the tree, Ruth called someone from town to come and do the job instead.

The digger strained. There was a ripping sound, like the earth unzipping. The roots let go suddenly and the digger wobbled on its tracks. As the machine reversed, the roots trailed behind, like a harrowed hand reaching out to Ruth from the grass.

§

The first morning in her shed, Ruth pulled up her chair and began her new routine with a brief meditation. She then smoothed a clean page, ready for twenty minutes of free writing. She was listening to the hysterics of a woodpecker and staring at the still-blank paper when she felt a lump beneath her feet. Toeing around, she dropped her head to see under the desk. The floorboards were buckling.

She pressed her feet firmly down on the bump, opened her laptop and picked up her phone to check her reviews again. They were still not good. I don't understand, Ruth thought.

Outside, the woodpecker's haranguing became louder and louder.

'No,' she told her phone loudly. '*They* do not understand.'

§

The following morning, Ruth went into her shed and found a sapling. A few sly inches of tapering wand poked up through a hole where the floorboards had now split. The concrete foundation beneath the shed had cracked and the sapling pushed out of the earth below it.

'Damn you.' She snatched at the sapling to tug it out.

Budding thorns nipped her hands as they slid straight along the thin twig. Outside, the wind picked up from nowhere like the high wheeze of a laugh.

When Ruth unclenched her hand, she found a pink graze along her heart line. She looked up 'hawthorn' on her phone: hagthorn, ladies meat, pixie pears, healing tree. *Oh please.*

She took a pair of scissors from the pen pot on her desk, and went to snip the stem at its base, but its fibres were too tough, too dense. By the time she'd located secateurs back in the house she couldn't face going back to her new office. She checked her stars on Goodreads and did some yoga for writers instead.

§

The next day the sapling was a foot or so taller.

Ruth's desk hopped from leg to leg, trying to balance on the strong stem pressing up from underneath. She got down on her knees with the secateurs, but the trunk was already so thick that she couldn't open them wide enough.

Ruth thought she heard someone chuckling outside and sat up quickly, catching a loose thread of her cardigan on a budding thorn and snagging it. But when she flung the shed door open, there was no one there, only a pair of coughing crows startled from the garden wall.

She sat back heavily in her ergonomic swivel chair.

Ruth, her mother wrote in a message in her inbox, *I haven't seen this book of yours in shops anywhere. Is it out or not?*

§

In the garage she found a saw.

The tiny blunt teeth found the sapling determinedly elastic but Ruth kept going until finally it collapsed slowly to the floor of the shed with one branch extended, clutching at the air.

She kicked the small tree out into the garden and peeled it apart, twig by twig, before folding it all into the mouth of her chiminea. Its infant fluids hissed and spat as she set the flame. She spent the rest of the day trying to capture this experience via all five senses in her observations journal.

§

On the third day, Ruth woke to an email from her agent enthusiastically suggesting a deadline. She was still in her pyjamas as she ran to the shed, trouser cuffs dragging on the dew.

The hawthorn tree had grown back voraciously overnight. It bent along the underside of the desk like a stooping giant, covered in tiny, threatening crimson buds. Well, she thought, as she piled up all the hardbacks of her first book that hadn't sold to weigh the desk down, at least it will be briefly beautiful.

She wrote with the tree between her knees, only occasionally stopping to push a heavy branch from her thighs. Her word count tracker was rising steadily until she received a text message from her mother.

Just checking – is an independent publisher a proper publisher, or do *you* pay *them*? Ruth threw her phone across the room. Turning back, she caught the bough of the tree in a punch to the stomach.

She shouted: 'Leave me alone.' But then felt what seemed to be the consoling hand of a twig lying across her thigh. She reached out to hold it, gratefully.

§

A few days later, the hawthorn had relaxed into a thin canopy. Ruth stood in the doorway of the shed. It was not a big space to be sharing with a tree that had now doubled in size. It's a matter of perspective, she thought. Plenty of people like trees. Plenty of people would love a tree in their writing shed. Plenty of people would consider this tree a feature.

She moved the desk, a little more carefully, to relieve the trapped limbs; to give the tree some space. It sprang up. The excited branches flung apart, flicking her across the cheek with an effete flèche, and her carefully placed piles of books fell to the floor.

She winced and breathed deeply.

Her chair was now barely inside the shed. She sat, wondering how she'd close the door in the winter. Imagining a moody author photo taken in her new eco-space.

She reached out and turned off her phone.

Ruth typed determinedly as fresh shoots poked idly at her face. She could still just about see the screen through the scrim of her watering eyes. What more do you need? she asked herself, with her head tipped uncomfortably to one side. The deadline she'd agreed with her agent had passed, but she was heartened by the incisive work she was producing, the words issuing sharply from her to skewer the page.

Relieved, Ruth hit send, and heard a questioning hum. When she looked up, she saw a hornet crawl along a bough. I am blessed with a wonderful imagination, she thought, as she watched it crossing its legs, staring at her with beady, black, judgemental eyes.

§

The hawthorn matured quickly. Its ravishing bloom stank of rotting meat and the air was electric with insects. The 'L' key of her laptop had become stuck with sap. As she tried to tease it out with a biro lid, she received an email from her agent.

Perfect word count! Stop there until we've had a chance to speak! I have big questions about the whole—

The laptop screen went blank. Ruth pressed the power button, quickly, repeatedly, but nothing happened. She shook the computer from side to side. She turned on her phone with sweating hands to call the manufacturer – to find out what might be lost, what might be recovered – and received a text from her mother.

Finally found a copy of yr book! Thicker than expected! Too big for bag. Will have to buy another time.

Ruth dropped heavily to her chair.

A warm breeze hushed through the hawthorn's white cap. Ruth bared her teeth and reached through, taking hold of the tree's neck, shaking it as hard as she could. Soft white petals fell, clinging to the sticky spittle of her lips, catching in her nostrils on each vicious inhale.

When Ruth calmed and pulled her hands out, they dripped blood onto the laptop. She felt her forehead hit the keyboard and slip from the slick keys onto the desk as she passed out.

§

Ruth came round, aware that she was typing somehow, that the laptop had strangely revived. The room was dark, the window blocked by the tree, its branches twisting up around the walls and across the roof. In the soft glow of her monitor, the shed had become a shining green firmament pricked with white stars and tiny, red planets. Her desk was wrapped in twigs and leaves and the keyboard gleamed with her blood: each key pierced with a treacherous spike.

The phone lit up with a new message.

Do you remember Fiona? Her daughter is a bestselling novelist! I said you probably wouldn't know each other. Let me know though!

Ruth examined the keyboard. She tested the ruthless tips, wincing with each tiny stab, interrogating each startled finger, as letters spread painfully across her screen. Thorns start out as branches, the internet had told her, then harden into a defensive point that cannot develop leaves or flowers.

Ruth had no room to sit up straight, so she coiled low to start typing again. She found focus in the pain, reopening the cuts on her fingertips, one word after another.

§

Not long after Ruth sent the final pages of her second book to her agent there was an auction. It went to the highest bidder, a large publisher, and one day the contract arrived. As Ruth looked it over, she received a text from her mother.

Another book! I still haven't read the last one ☺.

Read it or don't read it, Ruth typed, sloppily, unable to feel through the hard bark that had formed over the tips of her fingers. *But just so you know, it's all about you.*

That summer, the hawthorn tree burst through the roof. In the sunlight it was laced with orb webs and ruby-jewelled with haws. Birds sang in its branches, and the wind soughed through its leaves.

'You're Wasting Your Time' and Other Things I Tell Myself

BENJAMINA ALBANESE

I t's a warm Thursday evening in July. The sky is oppressively blue and I'm already late, trying to find a space in the tiny carpark. *<<You should have left work earlier.>>* My day job is managing the admin at my family's business, and because I start later than the other staff, I always feel guilty leaving early. *<<You don't deserve to leave before everyone else.>>*

In desperation, I rev the back wheels up over a curb towards a large patch of empty pavement, and hear scraping as the front of the car tries to follow. *<<You saw the high curb, why did you park here?>>* Cringing, I grab my bag, lock the car, and run to the large, wooden doors of Toxteth Library. They're locked. Why do I always do this to myself? *<<Because you don't learn.>>*

At twenty-eight, this is the third writing group I've attended, and the first since coming out. I knock gently on the doors *<<Don't disturb them>>* and can't help wondering whether this is a sign. << *They'll think you're terrible. Just go home.* >> Reminding myself why I'm there, I knock louder. A man opens one of the doors. I can't run now.

'I'm here for the TranScripts writing course,' I say and wait for him to tell me they've already started and I can't join.

Instead, he smiles and ushers me in. 'I hope you haven't been waiting long?'

I shake my head; he has no idea.

I was twenty-one when I went to my first writing group. I arrived late for that one too and wasn't even sure I was at the right place. << *You can't go in there. You'll interrupt them.* >> For over twenty minutes, I stood staring at closed doors on the verge of tears. << *You're pathetic.* >> I genuinely don't know how I managed it, but eventually I did go in and listen to the work of people I assumed were better than me. << *They're real writers.* >> When asked if I wanted to share something, I scrambled through a folder and read a section of a children's story I'd never read to anyone. They were polite, but I was totally overwhelmed and felt like a fraud. << *You're not good enough.* >> I never went back.

Once inside Toxteth Library, I walk through glass doors into a cavernous room and join the TranScripts group. Avoiding direct eye contact with the dozen or so faces, I take an empty seat near the door. I struggle with names at the best of times and I've missed the introductions.

'Can you tell us a bit about yourself?' asks Marj, the facilitator, looking directly at me.

Shit. I'm sitting in a room surrounded by strangers and books, and all their attention is on me. << *Why did you sign up for this?* >> I mutter something and hope they don't all hate me already. The shelves of books gnaw at my resolve. <<*Mum was right. You'll never be a writer.*>>

Two years previously, my mum died and I stopped writing. She was my main creative driving force. Not because she encouraged me to write, but because she didn't think anyone could survive as an artist. In fact, the one time I talked to her about wanting to be a writer, she told me to 'Be realistic. It's only people who are very talented or very lucky that are successful.' That was my mum: realistic, down to earth. Creative, but only when it was socially acceptable, like making cards for birthdays.

I wanted, desperately, to prove her wrong. I wanted to show her not only that I could be an artist, but that I could also be happy and fulfilled.

In the library, I'm given a ten-minute exercise and the opportunity to share what I write at the end. <<*You can't refuse.*>> I put my pen on the page. <<*They're going to judge you by this.*>> I lift my pen off the page. I can't do it. <<*They wasted this spot on you.*>> I'm incapable of sharing my imperfect, messy self with this group. <<*What convinced you to actually turn up?*>> I remember all the times I've been too scared to communicate. The GCSE English exam where I didn't write a word for the first hour; the emails and messages I never replied to; the university coursework I couldn't ask for help with; and all those conversations I avoided having with my mum. So I make a decision. I will get through this one class and then I will drop out. It's too much. I admit it. I tried and I failed. The inner critic has won. Yet again.

The last thing I'd written before that TranScripts workshop was a Mothers' Day gift; a poem I inscribed in a card I made myself. It was the last gift I gave my mum. <<*It's not perfect.*>> No, and that didn't matter. It was enough that I tried and shared it with her while she was still with me. She loved it.

Sitting with the TranScripts group, I look around the room; everyone has their heads down writing. I'm scared of them, but I somehow see that each of these strangers is a person, with their own insecurities and fears. They're made of the same things I am – parents, the desire to write, hope for a more accepting world – and they're still here, writing and sharing. If they can, why can't I? In that moment, I realise that voice holding me back is made of my own thoughts, and for the first time, I silence those thoughts consciously.

I stay for the whole workshop. And more than that, I keep going back and complete the course. I become part of the group and begin to learn how to share the words I've hidden for so long.

When you bring yourself to the surface, no one remains a stranger for long. I joined a queer women's book club with Claire, and an LGBTQ+ writing group with Ratte. Marj, who welcomed me, inspired and encouraged me to shape a new creative life so that, in 2021, I left the office job I'd spent my adult life doing and finally started calling myself a writer and an artist.

After TranScripts ended, I was published, and got through my first four performances in just a month. All of which terrified me, but I decided to stop listening to the doubt that had always controlled me. I was learning to shape my life according to what I was passionate about, regardless of the fear.

Connecting with people through creativity is an intrinsic part of my identity that I will continue to explore while I'm able, daring to be vulnerable and supporting others to do the same. I write, act, absorb as many stories as possible, and collaborate with brilliant people. Dreaming radically. Sharing openly. Living true to myself. My life may be wild, messy, and unconventional, but now I'm not only surviving, I am thriving.

The truth is that the voice will always shadow us. Mine grew louder when I started writing this essay, trying to tell me I couldn't do it, but it no longer holds the same power. However we wish to express ourselves – making birthday cards, writing essays, performing on stage – we are, and always will be, artists. So now this essay exists, a reminder for me and for you: don't let anyone, not even yourself, convince you that your voice isn't valuable. Art transforms lives, and the world is waiting for yours.

Inner Critic

Name the inner critic.

Naming your inner critic creates a gap between you and it. You learn to differentiate between the wise nurturing voice inside and your internal critic. *Oh, there goes Patty again.* You can then choose not to listen. Every time Patty (or whatever you name your critic) pipes up, practise channelling Ru Paul and say to your inner saboteur: Thanks for sharing, but no thanks. And then go to the feeling underneath with buckets of compassion. What's wrong? Where does it hurt? What are you scared of? At the root of all blocks lies fear.

Meditate.

Sitting and breathing for fifteen minutes or ten minutes or any minutes a day really makes you a better writer. This is because you're training yourself again and again to come back to the present, to the here-and-now. This skill then helps you to let go of dreams of success, nightmares about failure and sweats about what other people will think – and to instead return to this page, this paragraph, this sentence. Meditation makes you less reactive and more reflective and works to widen that space between you and your inner critic.

Morning pages at any time.

Julia Cameron's instruction to write three pages every morning – of whatever comes to mind – is solid gold. Ask the millions of people who do it every day. I approach it a little differently: I write my pages before I start on my main project, whatever time of day it is. It's a lovely way of getting those critical thoughts out of your head and onto the page. Elizabeth Gilbert uses her pages to engage in a direct dialogue with her wise, compassionate self. Sometimes I do that or sometimes I allow the inner critic to get all its shit-talk onto the page then I tear that page out, scrunch it up and start writing. In this way I can begin to play on the page without the inner critic heckling me.

Writing Practice

Finding My Writing Practice

SARA JAFARI

My debut novel, *The Mismatch*, was born while I was on Faber Academy's 'Write a Novel' course. I had written a novel and a novella previously, both as a teenager, but once I graduated university it felt so much more difficult to sit down with my laptop and write a long piece of work. Years passed and while I would write short stories, I hadn't seriously considered writing another novel. It was only when I was going through a hard period with my mental health, and during a trip to Amsterdam with my mum, that I really started to interrogate why I felt so empty and listless. The first half of my twenties were spent feeling as though I had no idea what I should be doing with my life. Many of my friends had moved away from London, and I wasn't happy with how my life was looking post university. I had struggled for years to get a job in publishing and lived in a crumbling flat. I very much felt like:

is this really it? Is this what life is? (I am by nature quite dramatic, so it probably wasn't quite *that* deep.)

Walking along the canals with my mum in Amsterdam, I was barely taking in the beauty of the city. One morning, in our hotel room while my mum was getting ready for the day, I distinctly remember scrolling Twitter and seeing a children's author documenting the nitty-gritty realities and processes of being a published author. Reading about the struggles she'd faced as well as the highs opened a door to what I'd perceived as a mysterious process. I realised that part of the reason for my listlessness was that I had a dream that I wasn't pursuing. Seeing that author being so open about all of it made the dream feel more achievable, somehow. I'm a glass half full kind of gal, so even learning about the practical struggles of fitting in writing alongside a full-time job gave me hope that people aren't just born authors, they work hard to *become* them. And I knew I could work hard.

So it was then, in that hotel room in Amsterdam, that it finally clicked that I really wanted to give myself a shot at writing a novel, instead of just dreaming about it. But I knew I needed structure and guidance to help me achieve it. Enter: creative writing courses. I applied to do an MA in Creative Writing at a few universities, as well as to Faber Academy, and ended up being offered a place at all of them. My employer at the time declined my request to work four days a week, and as the Faber Academy course was once a week in the evenings, it was decided. It wasn't cheap – in fact it was the most expensive thing I had ever bought myself – but there is something about dropping such a large sum of money on your passion that makes you bloody well do it. It gave my writing a sense of urgency – I felt I really needed to write my book during the six-month course to justify the investment. It was painful seeing the money leave my bank account, but I remember thinking there was nothing else I would rather spend the money on. In the back of my mind, I thought I would see that money again in the form of a book advance, maybe even more than the money I spent (which I did). And it was during that six month course that my listlessness waned, and for that alone, it felt so worth it.

Once I was on the course, and after I decided what the story of my book would be about (this took at least a month – originally *The Mismatch* was going to be told from the point of view of five family members, a very different book than it is today), I had to decide how to carve out the time to write it. I was working as an editorial assistant full time, and living in a house share with one friend (not the flat in which everything was crumbling and breaking – I had finally moved into a place in a better state). Because I wanted a draft of my novel finished by the time the course ended, I set myself the goal of a weekly word count. Recommended to all writers is Stephen King's *On Writing*, in which King advocates writing every day. During my time on the course, I often heard of other students writing on their commute to work, or in their lunch breaks. Whenever or wherever you're doing it, the general idea is the same – that you write a set number of words every single day, or write for a set number of hours. That way you ensure you're getting closer to your goal. This idea is drummed into writers' minds as something you must do, even if it's only a paragraph, even if the sentences aren't particularly good.

When I wrote *The Mismatch* I didn't strictly follow this advice. Writing – like most things in life – really isn't one size fits all. The thinking behind writing every day is that it's a way to make writing engrained into our habits, and keeps the story and world you've created always stirring in your mind. But as with most daily challenges (thirty-day squat and ab challenge, anyone?) it's very easy to fail. How many of us have begun NaNoWriMo with so much steam in the first week, only to miss a day or two in the second, before giving up entirely, vowing to try again next year? Very quickly I realised a different approach was needed to make writing sustainable within my life.

The approach that worked best for me was to dedicate a few hours every weekend, with the aim of writing 5,000 words per week. Personally, this was more achievable than writing every day because my day job involved a lot of reading and I found by the evening the last thing I wanted to do was work with words again (even if they were my own). One of the many pieces of valuable advice on the novel-writing course was from my tutor Joanna Briscoe, who stressed to us the importance of seeing our writing as a priority and being clear with loved ones that we couldn't move our writing around; that is was important to stick to the time we'd set for ourselves to write.

I'm not *that* strict with my writing, but I found that giving myself a full week to hit a word count, rather than a single day, gave me the flexibility to make up for any missed writing sessions. During this time, I treated writing as an event, and I arranged my social life around it, rather than the other way around. I'd encourage other writers to take this approach when focusing on a project: by prioritising your writing, you are in turn prioritising yourself. And you deserve to be prioritised.

So, once you have the schedule out of the way – a word count you want to hit daily, weekly, or even monthly – where is optimal to write? Back then, I wrote in coffee shops near my flat, or if my housemate was out, in the living room on the sofa or at our tiny dining table. I didn't have a fancy writer's desk (our flat was certainly not big enough!) – but looking back, there was something freeing about this way of working. It was just me and my laptop, writing wherever I could and wanted to. Often, I'd write in bed past midnight, which is where I find my creative juices are at their purest. It reminds me of being a teenager and writing fanfiction and stories in bed with my clunky Acer laptop. There is something about night-time that really loosens your writerly inhibitions. Everyone is asleep, your phone isn't going off, there are no errands you can run – plus, you can be in your pyjamas. For me, the biggest perk of writing is that you can do it wherever you like. Part of this essay was written on my mobile when I couldn't sleep, other parts in the daytime at a Pret, or on my sofa in the evening. Embrace this chaos – also known as flexibility – because there really is no perfect way of writing, only what works for you.

§

Writing and publishing a novel is a long process – the work doesn't end when you finish the draft, or even when you find an agent, or publisher. When it came to revising *The Mismatch* with notes from my editor, I had started going to Caffè Nero before work every day and spending around thirty minutes to an hour editing and writing new scenes. When you're under contract with a publisher you have specific deadlines to meet for returning each draft, and I found my weekly word count approach worked less well – I had too much detailed work to do and I wanted to take my time with it. Like with writing later at night, I found that writing early in the morning meant I wouldn't be bothered with messages, and I could be similarly productive. There is also something really special about showing up for yourself every morning – for the first thing you do to be for you, and not for your nine-to-five job.

While it wasn't an approach that worked for me when writing my first book, when I'd finished my editing for the day, then went into the office, I felt like letting out a long breath of relief – because I knew I'd done something important to me, all before 9 a.m.

§

For my second book, which I began writing in 2020, I took a different approach again. Sustaining a writing practice during a global pandemic was an interesting one – especially when I was contracted to write the book by a publisher. In this situation you can't take all the time you would like to, and the pressure becomes very real.

As we all know, the world drastically changed in 2020. I'll hold my hands up and admit that I missed the deadline for the first draft of my second book, by about five months. Like many people, the events of 2020 completely derailed my sense of self, and writing took a back seat as a result. For me, writing can be an escape. When everything was on fire around me, I found it incredibly difficult to allow myself that escape. I also found I couldn't juggle all the things I had attempted to juggle before. Working full time, running a magazine, editing *The Mismatch* and writing a new book, all while doom-scrolling and with family members in Iran contracting coronavirus and my anxiety spiralling . . . In this situation, I chose to drop something, and that thing was my writing. Perhaps that choice sounds like the wrong one, or something I should have felt guilty about – but I didn't, and I maintain there's nothing wrong with that. It's so important to give yourself a writing routine – but not at the cost of your mental health. Giving yourself a break is a necessity.

When I eventually returned to writing my second novel, I followed King's approach of writing every day – to catch up with my approaching deadline. It was November 2020, and we were in what was meant to be a 'circuit breaker' lockdown yet would extend well into 2021. It was also NaNoWriMo, and I had decided to write a good chunk of my book during this time with two friends who were also taking part. We would motivate each other every evening over WhatsApp, often timing ourselves for an hour and updating each other on how we did in sixty minutes. Those winter evenings were spent on my sofa listening to Phoebe Bridgers or Taylor Swift and writing furiously to their dramatic beats. This practice not only distracted me from world events, but also reminded me of the beauty and power of writing, and why I fell in love with it in the first place. While I didn't write 50,000 words that November, I did write around 30,000 . . . Words that I later scrapped completely. They weren't wasted words, though. Writing consistently for a month pulled me back into the world that I created, and helped me develop my characters. I hadn't felt that connection towards my writing in a long time.

As long as you can avoid beating yourself up for not achieving certain goals, having them, and even partly meeting them, still gets you closer to your novel. As with any journey, there will be bumps along the way – and that is more than normal. My advice would be to expect them and adapt when you hit them. Then: keep on going.

No one can physically write your book for you. No one will be checking up on your word count. Unlike on TV and in the movies, you won't have agents and editors begging you for pages. That isn't realistic, and even if it was, it has to come from you first – your writing is yours, it really is just you and your computer. That means that fundamental to any writing practice is keeping yourself motivated and committed to writing. You have to think of your *why*. Why do you write?

For me, I began writing to see myself in stories. The books I read growing up were populated by people who didn't look like me. I never read about British Iranian Muslims or their families. Things have improved since then, but British Iranian stories are still thin on the ground. So I write for myself, and for others who want to relate to a character like them with a similar background and history.

I also learn so much about myself as I write. It's therapy. I feel a weight lifted after a good writing session. Sometimes, I don't even realise how tightly I've been holding onto an idea or feeling until it's on the page and I find I can let out a breath and move on. Or, sometimes, I realise with an urgency that it's something I need to delve deeper into, and that is such an exciting feeling. So, think about it – what's your why? Hone in on it. Remember it. Write it down on a Post-it note and stick it to your wall. Chances are your why is like mine: a need, more than a want. So indulge in it, respect that need.

Your why is what will keep you writing, and your practice is what will help you take it seriously and enjoy it. Whatever that looks like, trust your own routine – everyone is different and all that really matters is that you write.

It's All About Loss

SHELLEY HASTINGS

It's the early morning push. Stacks of drafts, books and notes are piled on the desk next to the bed. You are propped up by your pillows. Your time is running out. You are writing about the rubbish that keeps gathering out the back. The ripped bin bags, chicken bones, stale bloated bread. It's bothering you, that mess. It keeps appearing on the page. But you don't know what it is or where it's going, and now there is a small high voice calling from the kitchen, *can you come*, and his head pokes round the door, his pyjama bottoms sagging. *Mum, the milk smells of sick.* You keep typing, *just give me a couple more minutes.* His sister calls him. You try to find your thread. You get up to shut the door and the strong coffee and optimism of an imagined breakthrough starts to sag.

You open Twitter. A young author you follow has written 10,000 words in a day. Tom Cruise is trending. There is a picture of him in aviators outside a curry house in Birmingham. His familiar face has thickened. Unless it's a lookalike; it's hard to tell. You zoom in and get that slack-jawed jittery feeling, time dissolving as you scroll. You look at your submissions sheet, check deadlines, fantasise about a retreat far away in an imagined empty room: wood floor, long windows, sea views. What you could get done in all that silence.

You can hear your son crashing around now, throwing spoons. They are arguing. *It's my turn now. Let go.* You look over what you have written. It's not working. You know it's all about revising, fine tuning, trusting your instinct, not giving up. But you can't bear to listen to another podcast about embracing failure. It helps to walk or swim or run. And to just keep at it, turning it over in your head. Trying to find the words that make you feel.

And it arrives, fleetingly, when you least expect it: a fragile idea, some heat.

A memory of you in the back seat of that coach, travelling upstream, shins itching, the banks of the motorway blurring past.

Or that cycle ride to Canterbury. You followed your kids down that long, winding hill, past the woman in the park spitting vodka. You locked up your bikes near the café. There was a dead pigeon, its splayed feet in the air like it was sleeping on its back. Your son was distraught, his face pink, lip quivering, *poor birdy poor birdy*. And that grinning man punting, with his shirt flapping open.

You had the kids' cycle helmets clipped onto your rucksack and they kept banging against your hip. You bought ice creams despite the fat raindrops and, afterwards, you sat sheltering underneath a wide plane tree as the kids licked the stickiness off their fingers and you took in the green splendour of the manicured lawn against the darkening river.

The bathroom door slams shut. *Go away. You're disgusting. I hate you.*

The television goes on.

You open a fresh page and start to type.

How to Hate Writing

KAYTE FERRIS

One of the worst things I ever did was decide to write 40,000 words in a month. My reasons for doing so were sound enough: it was a winter lockdown; I'd ended a long; unhealthy relationship; I was living in temporary accommodation; I was bereft over a boy. A nice chunky writing project felt like just the thing to give me purpose, to feel capable as my life was falling apart around my ears.

I also really wanted to get a book deal before the year ended – it was one of my official yearly goals and everything. I had been trying to come up with a book outline, yet every time I tried to corral the spark of an idea into chapters, it died. So it made sense to just write half a book in word count terms and then piece it all together into something usable. So simple, so clever; nothing could go wrong.

Of course, there were also reasons why it was a really bad idea: it was a winter lockdown; I'd ended a long, unhealthy relationship; I was living in temporary accommodation; I was bereft over a boy; and I badly wanted a book deal. These factors created a perfect storm where ambition and pressure met emotional and mental turmoil to explode in my brain.

And so here's what happened: I made a start. I made little boxes on the graph paper in a notebook – one box for every hundred words – and coloured them in with pencil as I went. I shared these boxes on my Instagram and people were interested in what I was doing and what it was for and that felt encouraging. Now I had public accountability too, so all the measures of peak productivity were being met. I had a list of one-word topics in a document and I would sit down, pick one at random, and start writing.

In the first week I wrote 15,000 words, but I also did no other paid work. In the second week, I had only written 1,000 words by the weekend and slogged my way up to 7,000 in an intense two days. Then, somewhere in the middle, I lost myself.

Because it's really not about putting finger to keyboard. That's what they all say, just write, just write! Just sit down and write and the words will come. And maybe that's true when you're not trying to write thousands of words a day, and maybe it's also true when you're not on the edge of a breakdown. The trouble is, when you sit down to 'just write' whatever is in your head when you're on the cusp of a breakdown, you spend your days confronted by everything that has contributed to that breakdown.

I observed my heart like a painter, holding it dripping and twitching in my palm, examining light and the shadow, noting where it was starting to die. My brain continually mining for whatever wretched story or emotion it could drag up that day, pausing and rewinding each moment, my hands on the keys trying to keep up with the endlessly flickering film reel. I spent all day steeped in everything that had gone wrong and was going wrong and then, for a break, I'd go out for a walk where the pounding of my feet served only to drum home the hopelessness.

§

Everybody thinks it is always raining in Wales, and sometimes we do get lashing rain or hammering rain or even trickling rain, but mostly it's that the air is wet. Sodden clouds sag over the mountains like handwashed knitwear and, down below, we get the drippings and escaped evaporation. It was on such a day, on one of my walks, that I encountered a dead cow. She had been hauled onto a steel trailer and dragged back to the farmhouse, left outside while, I presume, they decided what to do with her.

She lay at the crest of a slope and so I walked upwards towards her as if toward my own fate on the steel sacrificial slab. It seemed impossible she wasn't breathing, she was too big, too mighty, too powerful. I could not see her face, only the pink wound of unravelling flesh under her tail which suggested she'd died while calving. I picked my way slowly by. It seemed distasteful, almost blasphemous, to look.

I could only think about death then.

I walked into the foothills of the mountain, where the path is barely marked and crossed with sheep tracks so you don't know which you're supposed to follow. But I didn't want to walk that day, I wanted to disappear. As the moisture settling on my cheeks mingled with tears, I sat on a rock and thought about how I may as well be dead. The coldness that had crept inside me from the cow was joined by the coldness from outside, the two meeting at the heart of my bones. It wasn't that I wanted to die, but that life felt a bit like death. I hadn't touched another human for two months. I was effectively homeless. I was leaking all my resources and I couldn't see what life was possible on the other side of this. I might as well have been dead... only, I had a word count.

I think I believed the word count was giving me purpose, but now I don't think it was the cow that made me think of death that day. In the process of excavating 10,000 words a week I had, without realising it, been hauling out buckets of my life source and emptying them onto a page where they dried up and died. I was hollowing myself out, and whenever life tried to replenish itself with a thought or feeling I pulled it straight back out as some excellent new material.

This is not the place to get into the ethics of meat farming, but in the most over-simplified way, that cow was killed by her work. Her only value had been to reproduce, that was her work – that was all she existed for, and it was what killed her. Now, it's not the same because she had no choice, nor, to our knowledge, consciousness of what she was here for. But there it was, graphically in the red smear of her prolapse: her purpose, her work and her death all being the same thing.

It is now seven months since I saw the dead cow. Two seasons have cycled through and we are at the cusp of autumn; soon we will be back in winter, and the air will once again become dampness. I am a different person now – I feel on a molecular level – than the one who met with the dead cow, but I can still see her clearly, if I want to. I am still unravelling what it meant to see her that day.

§

On the last day of February, I climbed a mountain. I had only started walking further than down the road in January, but then I climbed a 730m mountain and sang in the woods on the way back down. Late that night, I typed the remaining couple of hundred words for the project, coloured in the final square and felt nothing. I often wonder, when people say that their goal is to make a million pounds, 'What happens the day after you make a million pounds?' And really I know the answer, because it's the same that happens the day after you complete 40,000 words in a month – nothing. You are the same person, with the same problems (if not more), the same bad habits, the same loneliness, aches, insecurities. Only now you have a number in your bank account or your Google doc in my case. I was lucky that I had my new, deep love of mountain walking which picked up the baton of purpose and channelled it more positively. My favourite part of any hike is not reaching the summit; it is negotiating the mud and finding the right trail and watching everything get small. I do it for the process more than the result.

I have barely written a word since the end of the project. The whole thing made me hate writing. Well, maybe hate is a strong word, but certainly it made me fear it. Made me scared to excavate again and left me with a general 'I don't want to' about writing. The irony was that my New Year writing goal had been simply to write daily for five minutes or more – just because I wanted to, just for the love of the craft. But this wasn't 'enough', and my lovely little intention became infected by productivity, and metastasized into a hulking project that was for something.

Yes, in a literal sense it was *for* the development of a book, *for* creating some kind of body of work. But it was also for creating an objective, a usefulness, for my own life (and here again my thoughts drift to the cow, and the bloody unspooling of her sole usefulness). It couldn't be for the love of the craft, or to simply practice – there had to be a goal, a magnitude. It had to be defining; to write was to define me.

But what the project actually showed was that writing cannot be the thread your life hangs by. In that February the single thread was thinning, the strands separating and beginning to strain. Since then I have braided a stronger life with new threads of body nourishment, investment in friendships and moving deeper into the mountains, a woven tapestry as opposed to a raggedy thread. I balance on thin paths and crouch out of the wind and dip toes into stinging ice water and every time I know I am alive.

And writing is in there too. A shabby thread perhaps but I have started to run it through with gold, like a kintsugi plate – all the more beautiful for its breaks. It is a more measured writing practice now, based on what I find interesting, not what is excruciating, and not daily as I believed it had to be. It is a part of my life, not its defining feature and that, I think, is it. If you want to hate writing, really hate it, do nothing but write. But if you want to love it, then make your life a braid of multiple loves; the gold shines best threaded with colour.

Writing Practice

Make time to dream.

Believe it or not, you don't need endless amounts of writing time – but what you do need is dreaming time. If you're imagining, reflecting, taking notes on your story or non-fiction piece, when you sit down to write – even if it's only for twenty minutes – most of the work – the imagining – has been done. You won't have imagined all of it – that would make the writing experience boring – but just enough so that you come to the page with a sense of your story and the people who populate it. So dream and dream big.

Go slow and steady.

The tortoise always wins. Try to notice when you rush. What's driving you? Often, it's the need for affirmation and validation.

We rush because we want an end product, something to show for all this time we're 'wasting'. But when we rush, the writing will actually take longer because it won't be as rich, it won't be as fully imagined and, therefore, it won't connect with readers as well as it could. Slow and steady is always best. Make like a tortoise and take your time.

But don't take too long.

Be sure you're not tinkering behind closed doors, perfecting every sentence. That's writing for validation and affirmation too. In truth, what you're working on will never be perfect because we are not perfect. You won't know what connects with readers and what doesn't unless you share. We are flawed humans making flawed creations. You could edit until you're ninety and still miss something. Write, edit, get feedback, edit again – then send it out into the world. Dance to Beyonce and pour yourself a gin. You beat the inner critic.

CHAPTER 5

Be Courageous

Fuck (Your) Demons, Find Community, Become Incandescent

JANE CLAIRE BRADLEY

So you've found your voice. Or to put it another way: you've started to build your trust in that voice you've always had. You've clawed through the shit to get to the gold, and now you're starting to believe. Your writing needs to be shared. It's an ember glowing inside you, and either you dig it out to use as a lantern-light, or it burns you alive. You find your voice, and then you start to use it. And that's a thing that, frankly, can be fucking *terrifying*. Not just nerve-wracking or scary, but a down-to-the-bones beyond-words fear that sends *danger, danger* warnings storming through body and brain.

So we do what we've been taught: we censor and silence and diminish ourselves. Also known as: the most elaborate, invisible, poisonous, cruel and unjust bait-and-switch there's ever been.

Because not being heard can just seem so seductively *safe*, can't it? To not risk it, not face our fears, to not put ourselves in a position where we might be met with rejection, criticism, indifference, humiliation. People getting to glimpse our most hidden, secret parts: our dark, weird, messy, rotten, resilient and glorious minds and hearts and souls. Fuck that. Way too exposing. Better to stay quiet, cosy, polite, well-behaved. Slip by unnoticed. Safe.

Except.

Women experience violence every day. And it comes in many slippery forms, from the subtle, insidious and near-invisible to the most brutal and traumatic. It comes from partners, peers, strangers and the systems we live in. Women have been and continue to be murdered, tortured and burned alive as witches, for being poor, for living alone, for being healers or widows, for being queer or old or ugly or disabled. Think back over the past few years. How many women's names are burnt into your consciousness because they were murdered while walking home?

Now tell me: do you still feel safe?

As Audre Lorde wrote: your silence will not protect you. There is only one thing more frightening than speaking your truth and that is not speaking.

Here's some of how it went for me: A decade ago, I moved back to my home city of Manchester. I'd spent years in Leeds and then London, where I'd slowly found a few keys to the hidden hearts of certain subcultures; secret, pulsing places where everything felt raw and alive and important. Through that process, I discovered parts of myself I didn't know were there. I fell head-over-arse in love with live performance and spoken word, with queer punk and feminist activism, with squat parties and DIY gigs that come to me now in a swirl of howling guitars, distorted vocals, glitter, sweat and smoke.

During my last year in London, I'd become part of a makeshift feminist arts collective, and started producing events. Until then, I'd strictly stayed part of the audience: intoxicated, energised, envious and terrified. Simultaneously dazzled with admiration and sick with longing to be brave enough to claim those stages as my own. Even when I started putting events on, I never shared my own work. I could create spaces for other people to share theirs, but standing up and reading my own writing? My weird, stilted, perpetually half-abandoned stories that I knew were both too try-hard and too tentative, that just seemed derivative, dishonest and shit? Nah mate.

I moved back to Manchester, on the opposite side of the city to the Salford council estate where I grew up. *Maybe now I can become a real writer*, I thought. *With my living expenses so much lower than in London, I'll have time to commit to my craft.* I researched writing groups, and went to rooms in pubs and libraries and church basements. Passed round print-outs of my work and tried to pretend I wasn't dying inside at the prospect of having them read.

No-one ever told me how many frogs you have to kiss before you find your prince. No-one ever told me not to take my short story about shagging the devil in a cemetery to the group of lovely middle-class women in their seventies. One of them loved it, and gave a ton of insightful encouragement, but the other seven stared at me as if I was actually Satan and not just someone who fantasised about fucking demons as a creative pastime. I persevered for six more months, taking more and more toned-down versions of my work, but I always got told I was too out-there, too unsettling and unpublishable and not using grammar right either.

I stopped going.

There were other groups, but I always came out feeling the same: not good enough, not writing about the right things in the right way, and not even able to do polite writing chit-chat without exposing myself as too loud, too common, too political.

Parallel to all of this was me coming out, again, in the city I'd not lived in since my teenage years. Rediscovering the underground queer arts community and all its magic: the music, drag and art. An elevated, more multi-faceted version of that same joyful sense of homecoming I'd found in my earliest adolescent adventures into queer clubbing over a decade before.

I found a queer writing group, for 'emerging writers' under thirty. I was six months shy of being too old, and at first I grieved that I'd missed my chance. Then I emailed them anyway.

My first meeting, I was buzzed into a dark mouldy corridor beneath a Quaker House. *Just follow the music*, a voice had instructed me through the crackling intercom. I passed offices with padlocked doors, in the direction of a sleazy sonic beat and muffled voices. I found the chaotic headquarters of an indie publisher. No windows and books everywhere: in boxes, on shelves and in precarious towering piles. And there in amongst all this mess: a cluster of people at the end of a long table wearing an assortment of outfits ranging from bejewelled Indian sari to latex leggings, double denim, afro wig and bowler hat. All of them dancing to a rave track blasting from someone's laptop.

This was *much* more like it.

The de-facto leader of this group was a weekend drag queen who had the utmost reverence for the dark arts of performance and theatricality. *Part of our responsibility as queer artists is developing and sharing our voices*, they said. And that meant literally: if you wanted your writing workshopped, you had to stand up and read it out loud. The first story I shared was about someone being violently assaulted for being queer, then setting fire to a pub with the perpetrators inside. Had to exorcise my adolescent trauma and pyromaniac tendencies somehow, didn't I?

After sharing this story with the group, I sat back down, downed the rest of my tepid tea, waiting for the inevitable soul-crushing that usually followed. And then I got one of the most useful pieces of feedback I've ever received. *Alright. Good start. Save that version somewhere. Then do a new version of your document. Call that the 'performance edit'. Go back to the beginning and strip out everything that isn't completely necessary.*

No one had ever told me anything like that before. And the more I kept going to the meetings, and witnessing all our work evolve, the more I came to understand what should have probably been obvious to me from the start but wasn't: page and stage are not the same, and if performing is going to be part of how you make yourself heard, they'll both need developing.

At the end of that first meeting, the group invited me to a showcase they were staging in a few weeks. It was in the venue's biggest theatre space. The poet Jackie Kay was headlining. And I could be part of it too, if I wanted. But I'd have to learn my piece by heart, and *perform* rather than read it. The workshops and rehearsals that followed were a crash-course in making myself heard.

I'm not saying performance needs to be part of every writer's practice. And I'm definitely not saying that performing from memory rather than paper should be anyone's ultimate aim (there are a ton of accessibility issues within that stance, for starters, and I don't believe in introducing more barriers to an already vulnerable and exposing process). But it's something I never expected to be as transformative as it became. I learned how to project my voice. I learned how to use the rhythm, pace and tone of my speech to build momentum, tension and emotion. And I learned a ton about embodiment, about harnessing the adrenaline rocketing round my system and using that as fuel each time I took to the stage to make my performances more hypnotic and exciting.

Even more valuable than these craft elements was that initial advice I received: go back to the start, and strip back. Because within that seemingly simple manifesto was a world of questions I'd never even considered. Which elements were the most important? What was I even trying to say? What did I want to leave the reader or the audience with? And why did that matter? When it was distilled down, to its purest form, why did I want it shared?

For me, this is the crux of being heard, the foundation from which everything else comes. You have to believe that what you have to say is worth sharing. You have to know your *why*. It doesn't have to be big or earth-shattering. But it has to *matter*, to you more than anyone. Whether it's because you want to rage against the world; share your most secret, precious joys, heartbreaks or shame; connect to a community; highlight injustice; be seen, recognised, accepted and celebrated for who and what you are. To tell a story, be it truth or fiction, and use your actions to advocate for your work. *I wrote this, and that matters. I'm here.*

For me, being heard was a practice like any other. It took time, energy and courage; it was and is an ongoing process of experimentation, development and refinement. It happened in the most miniscule of increments and in sudden massive shifts. And finding the people to do it with made all the difference. It's a long, ongoing journey, through sometimes dark and treacherous territory. I couldn't undertake it alone. Sometimes, the difference between safety and its absence comes down to the company. That writing group had many functions for me, but perhaps the most important was that it brought the fear associated with being heard into a tolerable range. Getting onstage was still scary, but there was also excitement and daft dressing room dances and an underlying unwavering loyalty and pride in each other that mixed in joy alongside the terror and made the latter so much more faceable.

Undeniably, the access to a source of peer mentorship, practice and accountability were incredibly important factors. But it was the mutual understanding, the common language and the *trust* that came from collaborating with fellow queers for the first time that transformed my confidence. There's a bell hooks quote that defines queerness 'not as being about who you are having sex with... but queer as being about the self that is at odds with everything around it, and has to invent and create and find a place to speak and to thrive and live.'

This was the permission slip I needed, to cast off the shame of continually feeling at odds with the everyday world, and celebrate the pure chaos, beauty and magic you can make when you start revelling in being outside it. Being in a group with drag performers, musicians and artists, all of whom seemed so secure and trusting in their ability and right to be heard despite their writing and art being (sometimes literally) balls-out wild and weird; these were the role models and co-conspirators I hadn't realised I'd been waiting for. I was coming to understand my own queerness not just in terms of my sexuality, but as a synonym for alternative, and other. For deviance, defiance, revolution, rebellion and transgression. For subcultures within subcultures and finding validation for all my glorious and furious ideas that had never before had a safe home.

Strip it back to the purest version. Why do you want to be heard?

To make magic, to turn the shit of the past into the strange and harsh and beautiful, and to be witnessed in that. To send up sparks so others can see me. *I wrote this, and that matters. I'm here.*

We did the show. There were storms that day, but despite the bitter winds and snow outside, we still had a full house. It was my first time performing onstage with professional sound and lighting, on the same bill as luminaries like Jackie Kay and Patience Agbabi. And in the chaos of chatter and celebrating after, one of the group pulled me aside. *We're going to Edinburgh Fringe in August,* they said. *You're coming with us, right?*

§

We took the train to Edinburgh together. Our first show, all of us at the venue more than an hour beforehand, fizzy with excitement and anxiety. By this point, I'd been gradually building my performance skills and confidence, but I was still only putting them into action intermittently. This was the first time I'd done any kind of performance more than once. The six of us were sharing rooms, sharing beds in rented-out-for-August halls of residence. We were absolutely spoilt rotten with options for other amazing art to see at Edinburgh Fringe, and we took full advantage, going to numerous things every single day, traipsing for miles back and forth across the city, unintentionally staying out until dawn. But all the while, we did our own shows each day. And in this context, surrounded by other artists at every waking (and sleeping) moment, with thousands of other shows taking place in adjacent rooms at every hour of the day and night, the entire surreal process became bizarrely normalised. Get up, eat breakfast, go see a gay accapella choir or some punk burlesque, watch a two-person play about intimacy and estrangement in a pub basement, pass a troupe of glam-rock pirates doing David Bowie covers, eat a picnic in an ancient graveyard. Be at the venue in time for your own show. Then more of the same: storytelling and dance performed against a projected backdrop of ethereal animation, erotic acrobatic cabaret, late-night dragged-up poetry and beatboxing. All of which to say: being heard can lead you to some strange and ridiculous places, places you never expected to be.

By our penultimate performance of that Edinburgh Fringe run, I was curled up in a far corner of the pub, napping under my cardigan until ten minutes to show time. The last one and I was almost late. Over the course of the run, I'd gone from being a wretched ball of pre-performance nerves to almost nonchalant. I'd built trust in myself and the others that I could share my voice and survive the process. That I could tell stories about shagging the devil – because I never gave up on that one: it got edited and remixed over time into what became my feature monologue in our showcase – by torchlight in a dark room full of strangers, and the world wouldn't detonate.

Habituation, repeated exposure, the way with enough repetition we adapt to anything.

I aged out of the group not long after.

A year later, one of the other members invited me to be part of a programme supporting women writers to write for the stage. A year after that, my first full-length play was in production, funded by the Arts Council. I started writing the story that would become my debut novel. The year after, I returned to Edinburgh Fringe, hosting and producing a sell-out run of a spoken word showcase platforming women and non-binary writers. That led to being commissioned to develop and host a year-long series of events at the Royal Albert Hall.

Perhaps it comes across like showing off to summarise it like this. As though it happened smoothly or by divine intervention, and didn't involve a *lot* of hours of self-doubt, stress, applications and spreadsheets. But this is part of what happens: you make yourself heard, you don't die, and that gives you the fledgling scrap of faith you need to do it again. And you keep building those skills: your craft and confidence and experience. You stretch and realise you're still alive and then you stretch some more. Your faith builds and starts to get louder than those historic, inherited poisonous whispers that say you'd better not expose yourself, disgrace yourself, show yourself up or let anyone see who you really are inside. You build your courage despite those voices. You are heard, even when everything inside and out is screaming that it'd be safer to be quiet.

There are many things about my identity that make me vulnerable to danger and violence: my gender, my heritage, my sexuality. I am protected and insulated by numerous vectors of privilege, and all these elements co-exist in a complex tangle, as they do for all of us. Am I entirely safe as I navigate the world? No. None of us are. But the act of being heard – however dangerous and vulnerable it sometimes seems – is the thing that keeps me from tumbling into an existential abyss of fear. It is the thing that reminds me of my own small power, the magical thread that keeps me connected, engaged and creating. I do it for me, for the strength and resilience it gives me, and I do it in tribute to that entire artistic ancestral lineage that came before us, to honour their courage and determination to be heard in the face of oppression and adversity. I do it for my community, to renew and re-spell and strengthen the bonds between us. I do it for the writers and artists still battling with everything they've got against themselves, their circumstances and their conditioning. I do it for all of us, and the web of protection and solidarity we weave when we advocate for ourselves, our writing and each other.

That ember inside me, I'd rather excavate it and use it as a light to guide me than allow it to burn me alive. That, of course, makes me more visible, and with visibility comes risk. But invisibility isn't safe either. *Your silence will not protect you.* Silence keeps you hidden: from yourself and from finding or creating the community who might just have everything you need. Sometimes, the difference between safety and the absence of safety comes down to the company. So I'm choosing being heard over hiding. And I hope that you will too. I want and need your company.

Home Made

CAROLINE GARDINER

You weave with words. Your keyboard clatters like the shuttle of a loom.

A café. A family at the next table. The mother's coat is cobalt blue. Two children, captured between stillness and running.

A golden thread spools from your hand, trying to outline your lover, who is not there, but twenty years distant.

The picture fades.

Delete.

The last time you saw him was in this café. The back of his cheap coat disappearing through the door. One last plea to stay. Was it him who said no? Or you who said: go then? Will he turn around this time and show you his face?

He has seen wonders. But you have seen only home, and hearth, and how will you pay the rent this month?

Cut.

The children of the family at the next table will not yet come clear. Their outlines ragged, their clothes the no-colour of bleached coral.

He did not want your children.

It was raining, that last time in the café. Steam on the windows. The waitress came over. 'Was everything all right?' She gave you the bill. He hadn't left his share.

But he'd left the door open. You shivered.

Starting again gets harder each time. The words are beginning to fray.

Now at the centre of the picture is the parcel he hands you like a surrender. A wine-dark waterfall of silk spills from the wrapping, out onto the café table, fringe like yellow seaweed hanging almost to the floor.

You do not want his dead mother's shawl.

This single piece of clothing burns brighter than everything else.

His mother didn't like you, so you hadn't expected to be left anything in her will. You'd read stories about jealous women giving poisoned gifts. You buried the shawl under the old sweater you never wore, but couldn't throw out.

Time is running out to get this right. Try again. Use your best words.

A rainy day. A busy café. A happy family. A tired waitress. A cold coffee. A deathly gift. A just-closing door.

The picture is still too dim.

Why is it so hard to make the words obey? They start off bright and certain, but always fade as soon as you begin on another part of the picture. It's impossible to hold everything in your mind at once.

The door is the hardest part to get right. The just-about-to-close-but-never-fully-closed door.

You could rewrite the door.

Let it be closed.

Your fingers fly.

Let him be hurrying away from the café through wet streets to the train. Its destination, twenty years lost.

And now the door is shut. Like the unstoppable ocean coming to shore, brightness floods the memory. The café gleams in gold, the children shine in lapis lazuli, and the shawl glows Titian red.

The door stays shut.

Shut down the computer.

§

'Sorry I'm late,' he says.

'It's all right.' I really don't mind. I'm enjoying watching the other customers. Thinking that the café has barely changed in twenty years.

'Did you order?'

'Not yet. I had to keep putting the waiter off. I told him I was waiting for a friend who's sometimes late.'

He smiles (a tooth is missing).

The waiter pounces. 'Would you like to order now?'

'Two coffees, please,' he says.

'I'll have tea.'

'You never used to drink tea.'

'I do now. One tea, one coffee, please.'

'Tea sounds good. I'll have one, too.'

The waiter hurries off, anxious to avoid further negotiations.

I take the shawl out of the Bag for Life.

'Here it is. To be honest, I never really go anywhere I could wear something like this. I thought your daughter might like to have something from her grandma.'

He fingers the silk, then puts the shawl in his rucksack. 'Thank you. It's a kind thought.'

The tea comes. We each take a sip.

'This tea is terrible,' I say. And we both laugh. It's amazingly easy.

I ask about his travels. He asks about my writing.

'I've started again,' I say. 'I've even sold a couple of things recently.'

He seems pleased for me.

The small bald patch on the crown of his head makes me sad.

'Well...' he says.

'You've got a train to catch.' We were always able to finish each other's sentences.

He grins.

The kids from the next table run around, loud with joy, and no-one seems to mind.

I pay the bill with money I earned from words I wrote, and I smile as the door to the street closes, and he walks away into the sunshine of a twenty-year awaited spring afternoon.

The Abandoned

DILLY ATTYGALLE

The day he walked out
of our home, our bed
is the day I found her—
I thought I had left her
for good, for dead.
She'd set up house
in the back of my head.
A dusty corner where
the light fails to enter
and Thought is caught
between musty cobwebs.
Where The Forgotten retreat
to wait till their dying day
knowing the inevitable fate.
When did she get here

which year, which decade;
it's hard to name dates.
Maybe between words—
'your clock is ticking'
and 'settle down for god's sake'
Maybe between roles—
the hostess, best dressed,
a homemaking goddess and
a damsel but unstressed.
Maybe between plans—
mortgage plans, career plans,
bullet journals and calendars
blocked for pilates but not
for pondering and play.
Maybe it doesn't matter how
she got here or even when.
Maybe all that matters is
there she was with eyes
tired but yearning, and hand—
her hand, still holding a pen.

Be Courageous

Engage with the world.

Go to poetry nights, go to book readings, lectures, workshops. Meet other writers, yes, but even more importantly hang out with people. All kinds of people. The introverts amongst us can use writing as an excuse to hide at our desks, but if you're writing about people you need to engage with people. Observe, listen closely, take notes on your phone, then go home and write all about it.

Experiment and play.

Experiment in different genres and play with different forms. But also play with other creative pursuits beyond writing. Whether you learn how to throw a pot or ice skate, any kind of creative act feeds into your writing and works to strengthen your creativity in general. You learn the value of process, not end result, by being creative with no end goal in mind. So play!

Forget about success.

Focus on courage. If you're focussed on success as defined by others then you'll always be frightened of failure – and that means you won't take risks, you won't be vulnerable and you'll always be tap dancing for others' approval. You also won't celebrate each time you skill up or finish something or share something because you'll be holding out for a future big win. Each and every time you sit at your desk and write, celebrate your courage. You deserve it.

Thank you

Thank you from Kerry

Thank you forever to Huxley and Danny for all the love and unfailing support. Thank you to all of my studvents for teaching me so much. And a huge thank you to my dreaming girl, Angie Kerr. Look what we did!

Thank you from Dear Damsels

We're in the habit of using the acknowledgements space of a new book to thank the readers and supporters of our previous book – and again it's true that *So Long As You Write* was born out of the unexpected success of the book that came before, *What She's Having: Stories of Women and Food*. For everyone who read and loved that book – thank you! It reached many more readers than we even hoped it would, and in doing so encouraged us to keep going with the passion project that Dear Damsels has always been – and to apply for the Arts Council funding that this book is supported by. Thank you, Arts Council England!

We've worked with more people than ever before in making this book, and we are so grateful to them. Kerry, we're so glad that the stars aligned for this project and brought our shared vision of a triumphant manifesto for writing to life. Thank you for being unfailingly supportive and encouraging and practical.

Thanks also to the wonderful Jo Myler, for the absolute gift of a cover – the Papier notebook of our dreams. And for making the inside as beautiful as the outside, thanks to Marcus Chamberlain – the thoughtful text design these words deserve.

And, of course, thanks to our writers: for opening your hearts and your notebooks and sharing the stories of what writing means to you.

Contributors

Jane Claire Bradley (www.janeclairebradley.com) is an award-winning writer, performer, educator and therapist, based in Manchester. Jane writes novels, short stories and performance poetry, mostly about teenagers, trauma, queerness and class. Jane's first novel, *The Summer Everything Happened*, won the Northern Debut Award from New Writing North. She is the author of a fiction chapbook, *Truth or Dare*, and has been longlisted for the Mslexia Novel Competition and the Lucy Cavendish Fiction Prize. Jane has performed at arts and literature festivals across the UK, from Edinburgh Fringe to the Royal Albert Hall, and is the founder of For Books' Sake (www.forbookssake.net), a non-profit dedicated to championing marginalised writers.

Luan Goldie is a writer and primary school teacher from east London. She is the author of *Homecoming* and *Nightingale Point*, which was longlisted for the Women's Prize for Fiction and the RSL Ondaatje Prize. In 2018 she won the Costa Short Story Award and her short stories have appeared in *HELLO! Magazine*, the *Sunday Express* and *The Good Journal*.

Marianne Tatepo is child 9/9 of a Littoral and West Cameroonian family. Born and bred in Brussels, she is based in London and works in book publishing as a non-fiction editor. Her fiction and non-fiction has appeared in the *Guardian,* the *Bookseller*, *Minor Lits*, *TOKEN* and *Brooklyn* magazine.

Sara Jafari is a British-Iranian author and editor. Her debut novel *The Mismatch* was published in 2021. She is also a contributor to the essay collection *'I Will Not Be Erased': Our stories about growing up as people of colour* and short story collection *Who's Loving You*. She single-handedly runs *TOKEN Magazine* as well as working full-time in children's book publishing.

Benjamina Albanese has always liked the word queer, and as a lesbian, trans, chronically ill brown woman living zero-waste without a bin, it fits her well. A Liverpool-based writer, actor and creative, she's passionate about exploring how stories are transmitted and persist through time, and enjoys experimenting with different mediums of sustainable, accessible communication. She will most likely be remembered for her climbing, faffing and skip-diving.

Caroline Gardiner has published a novelette for young adults, had poetry featured on London buses, dramatised ghost stories for audio books and created adventure games for the Natural History Museum. She's had short films broadcast on Channel 4, optioned by the BBC, and bought by Tate Modern. She was joint winner of the Jerwood First Film Foundation Prize for screenplays, and longlisted for the Red Planet Screenwriting Prize. In 2020, she was selected for the Spread the Word London Writers' Awards, and the Penguin WriteNow scheme. Caroline is currently working on a fantasy novel for children.

Charlie Rose Evans is 24 years old and currently lives in Birmingham, where she works as a receptionist for a trade union. Since graduating from Falmouth University in 2018, her work has been published on the Dear Damsels website and as part of the WriteThroughThis online anthology of young poets. This is her first publication in print.

Charlotte Turnbull's fiction has won prizes and appeared in *Mslexia*, *Litro* and *Barren Magazine* among others. Her work has been Pushcart-nominated, and translated into Italian. She was longlisted for the 2022 Caledonia Prize, and lives on Dartmoor with her husband and three children.

Dilly Attygalle is a Sri Lankan-born aspiring writer based in south London. She has written articles for various leisure magazines and her creative writing has been published on Dear Damsels. By day she works in publishing. Dilly is currently working on her debut poetry collection. You can find her on Instagram @book__affairs.

Elspeth Wilson is a writer and poet who is interested in exploring happiness from an underrepresented perspective and the power of writing to support mental health. Elspeth is currently working on her debut novel and also regularly facilitates accessible creative workshops. Her prose has been shortlisted for Canongate's Nan Shepherd prize and Penguin's WriteNow editorial programme and is supported by Creative Scotland. When she isn't writing or reading, she can usually be found near the sea or spending time with her elderly dog.

Emily Tucker is a primary school teacher based in north London, originally from the West Country. She writes teen fiction and poetry and has enjoyed being part of the Dear Damsels family since 2019. She mainly writes out of fear that she'll forget things in the future and a burning desire to immortalise every aspect of her silly life.

Katja Knežević is a Brussels-based poet and short story writer who writes in English and Croatian. She has published both poetry and prose in journals and anthologies, and in 2014 she won the Croatian national Young Poet Laureate award. In both languages, she explores themes of identity, trauma, nature and science.

Kayte Ferris – After a burn out, break up and burning down of an old life, Kayte became fascinated by the intangibilities we grasp for – certainty, knowing, what's 'right' for us – and what it might mean if we can never be sure. She creates, writes and podcasts about fulfilment, balance and redirecting ambition into a life worth living.

Safa Maryam is a 23-year-old daydreamer, sunset admirer and medical student (in decreasing order of success). She started story-telling when she was five and first turned to poetry to make sense of her feelings at the age of thirteen. Her work has been featured in Dear Damsels and *Mslexia*.

Shelley Hastings is a writer and producer. She is the winner of the Seán O'Faoláin Short Story Prize and the Aurora Prize for Writing. Her work has been published by *Southword Magazine*, Galley Beggars Press and Mechanics Institute Review. She is passionate about the power of the arts in dementia care, has worked for Age UK, and is currently running projects for dementia charity Resonate Arts. Previously she worked for over fifteen years as Artistic Associate and Senior Producer at Battersea Arts Centre.

What She's Having:
Stories of Women and Food

Food is about so much more than just the first bite . . .

What we eat can fill us up, satisfy our needs or leave us hungry for more.
It connects us to our culture, defines our routines and flavours our
fondest memories.

Whole stories are made across a dinner table, and in *What She's Having*,
sixteen writers explore the complex and meaningful relationships that women
have with the food we cook, eat and share.

A *GUARDIAN* BEST FOOD BOOK OF THE YEAR 2021

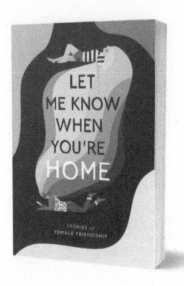

Let Me Know When You're Home:
Stories of Female Friendship

What is it that makes female friendship so special / complex / intense / important / messy / supportive / essential?

From growing up together to growing apart, from the oldest of friends to the fake ones, our relationships with other women can be our greatest loves. They can also be difficult, elusive and the source of our deepest heartbreaks.

In *Let Me Know When You're Home*, fifteen women writers look at female friendship in all its forms, in a collection of fiction, non-fiction and poetry that is both a frank exploration of these relationships and a true celebration of what women can achieve with the support of each other.

Tools for Surviving a Storm
by Nadia Henderson

In a transporting, original collection, Nadia Henderson examines the lines between nature and the human world through stories set in landscapes both brutal and beautiful.

Journeying from Sweden's ancient woods to the floodplains of the American South, the women in these stories navigate loneliness, loss and what it means to be alive in an ever-changing world.

Notes

....

....

....

....

....

....

....

....

....

....

....

....

Notes

Notes

Notes

Notes

....

....

....

....

....

....

....

....

....

....

....

....

Notes

Notes

Notes

....

....

....

....

....

....

....

....

....

....

....

....

dear damsels

your words | your stories | your collective

deardamsels.com

- deardamsels
- deardamsels
- deardamsels